I0760041

CAMP COOKING

Quarto.com

First Published in 2026 by The Harvard Common Press, an imprint of The Quarto Group,
100 Cummings Center, Suite 265-D, Beverly, MA 01915, USA.
T (978) 282-9590 F (978) 283-2742

EEA Representation, WTS Tax d.o.o.,
Žanova ulica 3, 4000 Kranj, Slovenia.
www.wts-tax.si

30 29 28 27 26 2 3 4 5

ISBN: 978-1-57715-656-7

Digital edition published in 2026
eISBN: 978-1-57715-657-4

Library of Congress Cataloging-in-Publication Data

Names: Harvard Common Press editor
Title: Camp cooking
Other titles: Camp cooking (Harvard Common Press, an imprint of The Quarto Group)
Description: Beverly, MA, USA : The Harvard Common Press, an imprint of The Quarto Group, 2026. | Includes index.
Identifiers: LCCN 2025030155 (print) | LCCN 2025030156 (ebook) | ISBN 9781577156567 hardcover | ISBN 9781577156574 ebook
Subjects: LCSH: Outdoor cooking | LCGFT: Cookbooks
Classification: LCC TX823 .C263 2026 (print) | LCC TX823 (ebook) | DDC 641.5/78--dc23/eng/20250707
LC record available at https://lccn.loc.gov/2025030155
LC ebook record available at https://lccn.loc.gov/2025030156

The content in this book was previously published in *Men with the Pot Cookbook* by Kris Szymanski and Slawek Kalkraut (Harvard Common Press, 2022), *The Family Camp Cookbook* by Emily Vikre (Harvard Common Press, 2022), *New Camp Cookbook Fireside Warmers* by Emily Vikre (Harvard Common Press, 2024), and *New Camp Cookbook On the Trail* by Emily Vikre (Harvard Common Press, 2024).

Design and Page Layout: Megan Jones Design
Photography: Emily Vikre: 30, 44, 51, 55, 56, 60, 74, 122; Hanna Voxland: 17, 18, 21, 22, 25, 26, 36, 39, 40, 43, 47, 52, 59, 65, 66, 77, 86, 89, 101, 102, 105, 106, 109, 110, 113, 114, 117, 118, 121; Menwiththepot: 69, 70, 73, 79, 81, 82, 85, 90, 93, 94, 97; Shutterstock: 14, 29, 32, 35, 48, 62, 98
Illustration: Michael Korfhage

Printed in Guangdong, China TT122025

GREAT COOKING OUTDOORS

CAMP COOKING

EDITORS OF THE HARVARD COMMON PRESS

CONTENTS

Introduction: Camp Cooking Basics 6
Let's Gear Up! 6
Camping Considerations 9
Stay Chill: Tips for Packing Your Cooler 10
Let's Cook with Fire! 11
Planning Your Menus and Hitting the Road 12
Keeping Your Food Safe While Camping 13

1
BREAKFASTS
15

2
QUICK LUNCHES
33

3
TRAIL SNACKS
49

4
MAIN COURSES
63

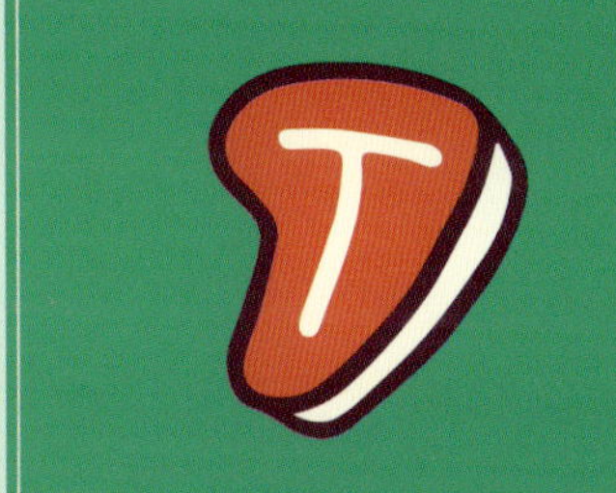

5
FIRESIDE DESSERTS AND DRINKS
99

Index 124

INTRODUCTION: CAMP COOKING BASICS

Camp cooking is a joy. Surrounded by nature, preparing meals over a fire or camp stove turns cooking into an adventure rather than a chore. It encourages mindfulness and presence, as you engage all your senses and truly experience the smell of wood smoke and the chill of an early morning while you brew coffee. Sharing meals with your companions around a campfire fosters deeper connections with them (and with nature), while getting away from home often inspires your appreciation for simple ingredients and cooking methods.

The recipes in this book are for cooking and gathering people around a fire anywhere. It could be out camping, but it could just as well be in your backyard, at a beach or park, by a grill on your apartment fire escape unbeknownst to your landlord . . . What matters is the sharing. This is not an instruction book on how to cook with fire. Those exist and are excellent references, if you need one. Then again, the best reference is giving it a try, watching your food like a hawk, and learning from experience. Even when you are cooking in a fully equipped kitchen, notes like cooking times are suggestions at best because every stove and pan is a little different. This becomes even more true when cooking with fire. So, using visual and smell cues are the best way to gauge your cooking. And test things as often as you wish to get comfortable. And, even if you incinerate things, you can always save the moment with some extra hot dogs and the fact that you are with friends. So call up some loved ones and pre-chop some ingredients, and let's warm ourselves and our souls by the fireside.

LET'S GEAR UP!

You can get very fancy with camping equipment, of course, but to start, here are some camp cooking must-haves.

Cooler

A good cooler with adequate ice allows you to have all sorts of fresh ingredients, making it possible to eat like a gourmand in the woods. There is a variety of coolers on the market now with superthick insulated walls that will keep food plenty chilled for three to four days at a time, if not longer. If possible, bring two coolers, one for food and one for drinks. This will allow you to keep your food colder longer as you won't need to open either cooler for as many things.

Camp Cook Stove

You could try to cook over the fire only, but that's basically inviting rain and logs that won't catch fire, or conversely a fire ban, and general disaster. Bring a cook stove so you can at least make your kids' favorites in a pinch. With a good camp stove, you can cook pretty much just as you would on a stovetop at home, with slightly less precise temperature control. Most camp stoves these days even have a self-igniter and built-in nozzle cleaners, and don't cause nearly the problems or cautionary tales of woe from camp stoves of yore.

If you're car camping, more is better, so consider bringing a trusty two-burner propane stove.

Whichever camp stove option you are using, make sure you bring enough fuel. If most of your cooking is happening over the fire, you can get away with one or two canisters for a weekend. But if you're planning on lots of cooking and feasting for a large crew of campers, you might want to have one canister for every one or two meals!

TYPES OF CAMP STOVES

Here are the general categories of stoves to consider.

Tabletop Two-Burner Stoves

The Coleman two-burner is the old faithful of camping stoves. There is a variety of brands these days, but as a general rule these stoves use propane canisters and the lid folds up into a wind screen. These have fairly powerful and somewhat adjustable burners, and they work in inclement weather. Take a look at some of the options online and buy one that fits your budget. If you want the specific Coleman your parents had with the white gas tank that you pressurize with a little plunger, these days it's called the "Guide Series Dual-Fuel."

Single-Burner Refillable Stoves

A lot of excellent camp cooking has been done over an old MSR WhisperLite, one of many lightweight folding stoves that use white gas or alcohol. If you want getting your stove started to be a big part of the trip, one of these stoves may be for you! But there are also some quite ingenious systems in this category, including the Swedish Trangia system, which uses a simple alcohol burner with a nesting system of aluminum pots. There are also some very nifty DIY alcohol stoves you can make from tuna cans! If you're going to be carrying your stove and fuel, it may be worth making some sacrifices for lightness, but keep in mind that some of those sacrifices may include stability, adjustability, and reliability. In general, these single-burner stoves are not for the average family camping trip. If you need to use one, definitely make sure you familiarize yourself with your stove's operation before it's make or break to get food on the table.

Single-Burner Cartridge Stoves

There are many types of one-burner cartridge stoves available that use disposable butane or propane cartridges, some with a built-in cooking pot system, such as the Jet Boil. These stoves are very easy to use, fast, and fairly adjustable. Most of them screw right onto the canister though, meaning the cooking surface is up high, and a precarious pot of boiling water isn't the best thing when there are kids around. So like the single-burner refillable, there's probably a better option for most family trips.

Biomass Stoves

There are a few stoves out there that are a sort of enhanced version of cooking over a wood fire, using twigs and careful air management. The Bushbuddy and Solo Stove are two good options.

Two Skillets

If you can swing it, bring two different sizes of skillets: one 10-inch (25 cm) and one 12-inch (30 cm). A 12-inch (30 cm) cast-iron skillet may be heavy, but it makes up for it by being able to cook darn near anything all while toning your biceps in the process. Cast iron is nice because you can use it on a camp stove, or over a campfire on a grate, or even sitting directly in coals. And they last forever. In fact, the best cast iron is vintage cast iron. Just make sure you never use soap to clean it. Scrape it out and rub it down, and it's ready to go again. Aluminum skillets with detachable handles are also handy for a lot of adventures because they are lightweight and good for plenty of frying or sautéing applications, ranging from pancakes to vegetables.

Two Pots

It's helpful to have one large pot for heating soup or boiling noodles, and a smaller pot for things such as rice, couscous, oatmeal, hot cocoa, and desserts.

Camping Dutch Oven

Not a necessity per se, but if you're car camping and you can lug plenty of stuff with you, it can be really fun to have a Dutch oven so that you can bake a cake or rolls. There's nothing that says, "I'm good at this," like whipping up a Dutch oven cake after dinner. And you might find that using a camping Dutch oven is way easier than you think.

The classic camping Dutch ovens are made of cast iron and have little legs and a rimmed lid that so you can pile hot coals on top of it. Dutch ovens are usually 10-inch (25 cm) or 12-inch (30 cm), and they can be shallow or deep. Having a deep one means you can bake with it or use it for soups and chili.

Camping Knives

You'll want a pocketknife for applications such as marshmallow-stick carving and pulling out the tiny scissors to make amusing paper animals as a source of distraction when dinner is still cooking and your kids are wondering why they can't watch shows. But, you'll also want at least one (if not two) larger knives for chopping ingredients and slicing cheese, and you'll definitely want the knife to have a sheath to prevent dangerous accidents and to make packing it easy. You can buy knives that come with sheaths, but you can also make a decent sheath out of thick cardboard and duct tape.

Cutting Board

Just bring one lightweight cutting board and use plates as cutting boards if more are needed.

Utensils Galore

You'll need utensils to cook and eat with. You can buy specialized camping utensils, but that's totally unnecessary. Just hit up a garage sale or estate sale and procure a set of all the utensils on this list, designate them as your camping utensils, and voilà, that's what they are! Here's a list of essentials:

- Knives, forks, and spoons
- Unbreakable plates and bowls of any sort.
- Camp cups! For all your imbibing needs. Most importantly, you'll need mugs for coffee. Coffee mugs also work fine for water, lemonade, wine, and cocktails, but you might also want to bring a few other cups that aren't coffee cups, plus a designated cup in a different favorite color for each kid in the group to avoid squabbles.

- Wooden stirring spoon for literally anything. With a good wooden spoon, you will find yourself well-near invincible in the cooking department.
- Spatula for flipping things such as pancakes
- Ladle (in a pinch, a big spoon can also work for things such as serving soup)
- Very long tongs for all fire-related cooking
- Can opener
- Grater
- Wine bottle opener and/or bottle opener (unless everything you bring is in cans or transferred to other containers, which totally works)
- Aluminum foil
- Heat-resistant gloves (like welding gloves) or oven mitts

CAMPING CONSIDERATIONS

Here are some more things to think about!

Water Storage and Water Treatment Options

Your camping trip won't last long if you don't have good water. You'll need it for drinking, cooking, and cleaning. Before you leave, make sure you know exactly what kinds of water options you'll have available wherever you'll be camping and plan accordingly. If you are bringing water, it's a good idea to bring twice as much as you think you'll need. Jerry cans, large water bladders, and water coolers are all good options for water storage. And they're useful even if you are at a campground with potable water because it means you won't have to be making a million trips to the water pump.

Ingredient Storage

Camp cooking with kids around is about a million times easier if you get as much prep work done at home as possible. Vegetables can be transported prechopped, spices can be transported premixed, and so on. A good set of leak-proof stackable containers is life-changing in this regard. It allows you to transport prepped meal ingredients and then store leftovers in the emptied containers so that you don't waste anything. Your containers don't need to be camping specific, just sturdy and tight sealing. But, in the camping department, Nalgene makes a variety of small containers that are fantastic for holding spices and spice blends or for storing small amounts of liquids if you have any special oils or vinegars but don't need the whole bottle.

Coffee-Making Setup

Choose your coffee setup, and make sure you have ALL the pieces you need for it (quadruple check), and bring at least three times more coffee than you anticipate needing. If your kids are young, they probably won't go to sleep until it is far past bedtime, they'll wake up throughout the night to ask where they are, they'll get up at the crack of dawn while owls are still hooting, and you'll be able to put on a cheerful face through all of it because you have enough coffee.

Dishwashing Setup

It's not the most fun part of cooking in camp, but cleaning everything up when you are done cooking and eating is oh so important for keeping the experience pleasant. And, in fact, kitchen patrol duty is an EXCELLENT assignment for older children. They'll feel so helpful! They'll make memories! Make sure you have a basin or large pot for hot water (get your water heating off to one side of the fire while you're cooking the main meal), biodegradable soap, and a scrub brush. Some people like to bring a scraper for scraping pots and dishes. If you have space, it can be nice to bring a little collapsible dish-drying rack, but we generally just bring a few dish towels (we use them for wrapping things during the transporting-to-camp process) and get things wiped dry right away. If your campsite doesn't have a specific place for dumping dishwater, make sure to teach the child—or adult—on cleanup duty how to toss the dishwater away from where you are camping and at least 200 feet (61 m) from any water source, dispersing it in a wide spray so it evaporates easily.

Fire-Starting Setup

Make sure the wood you are using is from nearby or purchased on-site so that you do not accidentally introduce invasive insects to the area. No one wants that on their conscience. Many campsites have a place where you can buy firewood. However, this firewood is usually in large logs, so you'll want to bring a small wood-splitting hatchet. You need small logs first. And good kindling. Make sure you also have a good way to start a fire, whether it's matches, a lighter, or a blowtorch (aka "Boy Scout matches"). It's also not a bad idea to bring one or seven of those paraffin and wood chip fire starters.

Other

It can be nice to bring a variety of other elements for creature comforts. Here are a few things we always bring:

- Tarp with ropes to hang over the picnic table in case of drizzle
- Oilcloth tablecloth for covering the picnic table
- Extra folding table for more surface area for cooking, eating, and setting up favorite games for the kids
- Comfortable camp chairs for relaxing by the fire
- Large tubs for keeping all your gear organized. It is helpful to have a sizable assortment of tubs so that you can use them to store your gear at home so it's ready and waiting for you when you and your family decide you want to get out of town for a weekend. In fact, this may be the difference between going and not going.

STAY CHILL: TIPS FOR PACKING YOUR COOLER

How you pack your cooler is as important as what kind of cooler you use. Luckily, there are some universally applicable cooler-packing tips that will make you look like the king or queen of chill.

1. Get that cooler clean! Hopefully, you wiped your cooler down well after the last time you used it. Then wash it down again before you pack it. It's always a good idea to disinfect it as well. Plain white vinegar works great for this.

2. If you can, chill your cooler in advance. The colder your cooler is inside before you pack it, the longer it will stay cool. To prechill your cooler, fill it with ice water about twelve hours before use, then drain and pack it.

3. Make sure all your food is cold as well. Prep as much food as you can and transfer it to sealed containers to chill before you go. Freeze as many foods as you can, including meats and soups, and pack these frozen. Oh, and make sure all your food is in waterproof packaging. No matter how well you chill everything, your ice will melt over time, and there are few things ickier than soggy turkey or hot dog–infused melt water.

4. Plan your packing. Map out your meals and load them into the cooler in reverse order, so the food for your last day is on the bottom, second to last day is above that, and so on. Keep dinner foods on one side and breakfast and lunch foods on the other.

5. Lay down reusable ice packs as your very bottom layer. Then pack your food, filling in all the cracks between with ice. Leave as little space for air as possible.

6. Make a separate cooler for drinks. Icy cold margaritas for you and fruit-infused ice water for the kids? Luxury! And if your drinks have their own little cooler, they won't have to compete with the kebabs for space.

7. In camp, keep your cooler in a shady place and open it as little as possible. The cooler you keep it and the less warm air you let in, the longer it will hold its chill and the better it will keep your food.

8. Don't drain the ice melt water. Science has shown that leaving the melt water in there keeps everything colder. But consider this yet another reminder to make sure all your food is in leak-proof, watertight packaging.

LET'S COOK WITH FIRE!

Campfires and campfire cooking are one of the profound pleasures of camping, if not one of the main reasons for going camping at all! You can proudly think to yourself, "I am human. I control fire." Just make sure you really are controlling your fire. First you need to know how to build it.

How to Start a Fire

Start with good tinder. Lots of paper, birch bark, or a fire starter is an absolute must. Do not try to start a fire without something that will catch fire easily. Next, make sure you have plenty of small twigs that will also catch fire easily. Be sure you have small branches or dry, split logs to add once your twigs are burning happily. If you rush to large logs, you'll smother your fire. So, kindling first, then twigs, then small branches, then small firewood, then finally add some small-medium logs. When the small-medium logs are burning well, add a large log or two.

If you start by adding your firewood in a teepee shape, once things are hot and chugging along in flaming fashion, you can chuck in more logs as needed.

If you can't start your fire with matches and all your kindling, it's pretty satisfying to hold a blowtorch up to a log until it succumbs, and you have fire.

Most campsites have a firepit or fire ring, and that is definitely where you should build your fire. Don't go rogue. It's not worth the fire hazard. If for some reason you find yourself in a situation where you need to create your own firepit, first make sure you are minimum of 30 feet (9 m) away from anything flammable, dig a pit in the dirt, then make a ring of large rocks around it to create a fireproof barrier.

Now We're Cooking!

Cooking food over fire is all about managing your heat and trusting your instincts about what is too hot, what is not hot enough, and when your food is adequately cooked. Cook times and specific instructions go out the window when it comes to fire, so you have to pay attention to sensory cues such as how your food looks and smells and make your decisions based on that.

Many campsites have a grate over the firepit, which you can use for putting pots on or use like a grill. But you may also want to provide your own grate so that you will be assured that you have one, and it will typically have grill bars that are closer together. You can buy a handy camping grate on foldable legs and tote it with you wherever your adventures take you.

You don't want to cook food over a high flame. Let your fire burn down to hot coals, and make sure you have accounted for the time this takes when you are planning your cooking start time. When you are ready to cook, you want to do what is called "grading your coals" in order to create different zones of heat. Using your long tongs or the best fire tool of them all—a long stick—spread your coals so that you have a thick, hotter layer of coals for medium-high cooking on one side of your firepit and a sparser layer of coals on the other side for lower-heat cooking. Pay attention to your food as it cooks. Does it seem like it's going too fast? Then spread your coals out more. Too slow? Pile the coals higher and maybe add another little piece of wood off to the edge to start to burn into more coals.

PLANNING YOUR MENUS AND HITTING THE ROAD

When you plan out your camping trip menu, think about what your family likes to eat and how much time you really want to spend cooking. There is no right or wrong answer: Just think about what works for you. On some trips, the best part may be cooking elaborate meals while you enjoy hanging out by the fire. On others, meals need to be fast and convenient because you're going to be mostly on the go. Or you might choose a mix where a portion of the meals are more cooking intensive while others are prepped at home and just need to be heated (or not even heated) and served. Plan your menus so that you use up the most perishable foods on the first couple of days of camping while later meals rely more on dried or canned ingredients. Also, there is nothing wrong with eating the same thing for breakfast and lunch every day. Finally, make sure you have a variety of bail-out meals such as boxed macaroni and cheese, dried soup for rehydrating, plenty of pitas and peanut butter, and lots of chocolate. There are few situations that cannot be saved with a hefty dose of chocolate.

KEEPING YOUR FOOD SAFE WHILE CAMPING

Be sure to research the requirements for protecting your food at each destination. It's not good for wildlife or people if critters of any size get used to finding their food in campsites. If you are van, car, or camper camping, you will likely need to store your food in a hard-sided vehicle or in a bear box any time you are not in your campsite. It's easy enough to keep a cooler inside your vehicle.

Backcountry campsites may have a bear box, or you may need to carry a bear barrel, which is a bear-proof, lightweight plastic barrel that comes in many sizes, and you either fit it in a pack or wear the barrel itself as a pack. Some areas may require you to hang a bear pack, which means hanging your food pack high in a tree so that bears can't reach it from the ground or from a nearby tree. If you're not familiar with hanging a bear pack, definitely look up how to do it before your trip. At the least, you'll need a long, sturdy rope or two and a plan for how to throw one end of the rope high enough in a tree. The ultimate bear pack setup is when you can throw a rope over a high branch on one tree and then the same rope over a high branch on a tree across a clearing. Then, you hang the bear pack over that rope using a second rope and a pulley. Very slick. A perfect bear pack is something to brag about when you get home after your trip.

Throwing a bear rope can provide a whole afternoon of entertainment. You need to have enough weight to get the rope up into the tree and over the branch. Just please don't tie your rope around a rock to get it over the branch you have in mind. The rock is likely to come crashing down upon your head or come flying out of the rope at just the right angle to nail a fellow camper. You probably don't want to tie your water bottle to the rope either. Instead, wind (not knot) the rope around itself to create a baseball-sized clump of rope just heavy enough to toss. As you throw the rope, it will, in theory at least, unravel over the branch and fall perfectly at your feet so you can tie on the pack.

Okay, are you ready? Let's go camping!

1

BREAKFASTS

Cherry-Pecan Granola 16
Coconut Oatmeal Bowl 19
Easy Breakfast Quesadillas 20
Eggs in Purgatory 23
Cream Cheese and Bell Pepper Frittata 24
Chilaquiles 27
Just-Add-Water Pancakes 28
French Press Dirty Chai 31

CHERRY–PECAN GRANOLA

YIELD: About 6 servings

Make a batch of this granola at home and pack it in a jar or sealed container to bring with you to camp. You can serve it with powdered milk or freeze-dried yogurt drops for breakfast, but it's also excellent sprinkled over cooked fruit for a dessert.

2 cups (180 g) rolled oats

1½ cups (150 g) roughly chopped raw pecans

½ teaspoon ground cinnamon

¼ teaspoon ground nutmeg

¼ teaspoon sea salt

¾ cup (241 g) maple syrup

3 tablespoons (45 ml) olive oil

1 teaspoon vanilla extract

1½ cups (180 g) dried cherries

1. Preheat the oven to 250°F (120°C, or gas mark ½).

2. In a large bowl, combine the oats, pecans, spices, and salt. Pour the maple syrup, oil, and vanilla extract over and toss well to coat—the best tool for mixing is your hands, even though you'll get stupendously sticky.

3. Spread out the mixture in a single layer on a rimmed baking sheet (it's helpful to line the baking sheet with parchment paper, but it's not necessary). Bake in the oven for 45 to 50 minutes, then remove from the oven and use a large spatula to flip the granola over in large pieces, trying to break it apart as little as possible. (Don't worry about some breakage, which is inevitable. You're just trying to minimize it so you can have bigger clusters at the end.) Return the granola to the oven and bake for another 45 to 50 minutes or until it is completely dry and no longer chewy if you take a bite.

4. Remove from the oven and allow to cool completely. Then break into the size of clusters that you like best, mix with the dried cherries, and store in a sealed container for up to 2 weeks.

5. To serve, in your camp bowl combine your desired amount of powdered milk or freeze-dried yogurt with some water to make liquid, and stir well. Add a scoop of granola.

1 packet (1.8 ounces/50 g) plain instant oatmeal

1 tablespoon (5 g) dried coconut milk

1 tablespoon (6 g) toasted shredded coconut

2 tablespoons (30 g) chopped dried tropical fruit such as pineapple, mango, kiwi, or guava (or a mix)

COCONUT OATMEAL BOWL

YIELD: 1 serving

If you like to start your day with something warm that requires very minimal time and effort, instant oatmeal is the breakfast for you. It will stick to your ribs, and it works as a blank canvas for any topping you can imagine, sweet or savory. This variation is a tropical medley in a bowl with sweet dried tropical fruit and aromatic coconut.

Try other combinations like banana chips and a spoonful of peanut butter, dried blueberries and chopped almonds or pecans, or dried strawberries and freeze-dried yogurt drops as just a few options.

1. Combine the instant oatmeal and dried coconut milk in a bowl. Pour about ½ cup (120 ml) boiling water over, stir, and allow to sit for 1 minute.

2. Top with shredded coconut and dried fruit, and enjoy.

TIP

In a typical grocery store, you can find *sweetened* shredded coconut and coconut milk in the baking aisle and *unsweetened* shredded coconut and coconut milk in the Asian cooking section. The good news is that you cannot go wrong with either. Choose the former for a sweet oatmeal bowl, or choose the latter to avoid the sugar, according to your taste preferences.

EASY BREAKFAST QUESADILLAS

YIELD: 4 servings

Have you ever noticed that a fried egg is almost exactly the same size as a street taco tortilla? Instead of going through the hoopla of first scrambling eggs, then adding them to a quesadilla, then frying the quesadilla, why not place cheese and a tortilla on top of a frying egg and save some steps? This may be one of the easiest and most satisfying breakfasts you can add to your roster.

2 tablespoons (28 g) butter, divided

4 large eggs

½ cup (58 g) grated cheese such as mild cheddar or Monterey Jack

4 6-inch (15 cm) tortillas (corn or flour, your choice!)

Salt to taste

Sliced avocado or guacamole and salsa, for serving

1. If you have a small cast-iron skillet, you can make these 1 at a time because they are so quick; if you have a large skillet, you can probably do 2 at a time. Place your skillet over medium-hot coals, add a pat of butter, and allow the butter to melt and foam. Crack in an egg (or 2) and sprinkle with salt. Sprinkle ¼ of the cheese over each egg you are cooking, and set a tortilla on top of each egg.

2. Cook until the egg is fairly set, 1 to 2 minutes, then flip each egg and tortilla stack so that the egg is on top and the tortilla is on the bottom. Cook for another 1 to 2 minutes until the cheese is melted. Then use a spatula to fold each quesadilla in half and transfer to a plate. Repeat to cook the remaining quesadillas.

3. Serve with avocado or guacamole and salsa. Feel free to add any other toppings you desire as well.

About 2 cups (490 g) of leftover pizza sauce or marinara sauce

¼ cup (60 ml) water

6 eggs

Salt and pepper

Fresh basil or parsley, chopped (optional)

Toasted bread for serving (*not* optional)

EGGS IN PURGATORY

YIELD: 4 to 6 servings

There's something about the combination of eggs and tomatoes that just *works*. The duo can be enjoyed in a variety of ways, but the evocatively named Italian dish *uova al purgatorio*, eggs in purgatory, is one of the simplest. While most renditions of eggs in purgatory call for you to whip up a tomato sauce before nestling in the eggs to simmer, try using the leftover pizza sauce that you might never use. This makes it into a super speedy 5-minute dish that is still wonderfully delicious. Depending on what region of Italy you are in, eggs cooked in tomato sauce can be mild or quite spicy. If you want a kick, throw in some red pepper flakes.

1. In a skillet, bring the tomato sauce and the water to a boil. Turn down the heat to a simmer and crack the eggs into the sauce. Sprinkle each egg with salt and pepper. Cover the pan and cook over low until the whites are completely set and the yolks are as set as you like them, about 3 to 5 minutes. By all rights, you should just cook the eggs until the yolks are hot but still runny.

2. Scoop the cooked eggs and sauce onto plates, sprinkle with herbs (if using), and serve with toasted bread.

TIP

No leftover sauce? No problem. Stir up a quick marinara by adding some garlic (fresh and minced or dried), dried oregano, dried parsley, salt, and pepper to 2 cups (490 g) of canned tomato sauce.

CREAM CHEESE AND BELL PEPPER FRITTATA

YIELD: 4 to 6 servings

The reasons to love frittata are many, almost innumerable. But here are just three:

One: Frittata is really fun to say. Especially if you roll your R, really give some explosive heft to each syllable, and then elongate the last A. Try it! *Frrrittataaaa*. You'll feel sort of like you're at Hogwarts casting a spell—probably to cause a chicken to appear.

Two: Frittata can be eaten for any meal of the day. It is good for breakfast, lunch, or dinner. It's also good for second breakfast, elevensees, afternoon snack, or with a cold beer while you're waiting for dinner to be ready.

Three: You can eat frittata warm, cold, or at room temperature and neither taste nor texture will suffer. If only everything were so easygoing!

Frittata is a great way to use leftover vegetables, so if you have any, throw them in there. The peppers and onions caramelize sweetly while the cream cheese melts into pleasantly gooey, tangy bites.

2 tablespoons (30 ml) olive oil

1 small yellow onion, chopped

1 medium or large red bell pepper, sliced into thin strips

¼ teaspoon salt

8 eggs

½ cup (115 g) cream cheese, divided into ½-inch (1.25 cm) chunks

---

1. In a heavy-bottomed 9-inch (23 cm) skillet, heat the olive oil over medium-high coals until it shimmers. Add the onion and cook until it has softened and become translucent, then add the bell pepper. Cook, stirring occasionally, until the pepper and onions are slumping, soft and golden brown along the edges, about 8 to 10 minutes. Stir in the salt.

2. Meanwhile, in a medium bowl whisk the eggs with the remaining salt. When the pepper has softened, pour the eggs over the vegetables and sprinkle the cream cheese on top. Move the pan over to a cooler area of the coals and cover the pan. Cook until the eggs have cooked through and just set on top, 6 to 8 minutes.

CHILAQUILES

YIELD: 4 servings

Can there be a greater endorsement for a dish than "it's chips and salsa for breakfast"? Chilaquiles, a traditional Mexican dish, is fundamentally fried tortillas coated in a brothy salsa. But for camping, you can use store-bought salsa and chips to make chilaquiles that are ready in a matter of moments! Topped with a fried egg, avocado slices, and fresh cheese, this is the most perfectly satisfying start to any day. But, it also makes a great speedy dinner, and you can easily swap out toppings for other favorites (think meats, beans, or veggies)!

2 cups (520 g) store-bought salsa (tomato or tomatillo, depending on if you prefer chilaquiles rojos or verdes!), at whatever level of spiciness your family likes

¼ cup (60 ml) water

8 cups (208 g) tortilla chips

1 tablespoon (14 g) butter

4 eggs

Salt

Avocado slices, queso fresco, and cilantro for serving (optional)

1. In a large skillet over medium-high heat, bring the salsa to a simmer. Stir in the water to loosen the salsa, then simmer for about 2 minutes.

2. Add the tortilla chips and stir well to coat, then cook until the chips are warmed through, 2 to 3 minutes. Transfer the chilaquiles to plates.

3. Return the pan to the heat and add the butter. When the butter has melted and foamed, crack in the eggs. Sprinkle with salt. Fry the eggs to your desired level of doneness, then slide an egg onto each plate of chilaquiles.

4. Add avocado, queso fresco, and cilantro (or other toppings!) as desired.

JUST-ADD-WATER PANCAKES

YIELD: Enough mix for about 40 pancakes

While sometimes it feels like too much trouble or a waste of fuel to cook up a hot breakfast, some days you simply can't get going without it. And pancake mix is the perfect thing for those days. This mixture is easy to batch at home and stores for months. Portion out and pack just the amount you need for your trip, and when a chilly morning rolls around, all you have to do is add water and fry!

4½ cups (563 g) all-purpose flour

¾ cup (90 g) dry powdered milk

⅓ cup (67 g) granulated sugar

2 tablespoons (30 g) baking powder

1½ teaspoons (9 g) salt

1 teaspoon baking soda

½ cup (80 g) small dried fruit such as dried blueberries or currants (optional)

Butter or cooking oil for frying

Maple sugar or maple syrup for serving (optional)

1. To make the mix, combine all the ingredients except the butter/oil and whisk until fully mixed. Store in an airtight container for up to 6 months.

2. When ready to use, measure out the desired amount of mix into a mixing bowl: 1 cup (156 g) of pancake mix makes about 4 to 5 pancakes. For every 1 cup (156 g) of pancake mix, whisk in ¾ cup (175 ml) water, until just combined. (It will still be slightly lumpy. Don't overmix.)

3. Heat a cooking pan or griddle over your burner over medium heat and add butter or cooking oil to coat the pan. Scoop scant ¼-cup (39 g) scoops of the batter into the pan. Fry until bubbles appear and the edges look browned, about 2 minutes. Flip the pancakes and cook on the other sides until golden brown. Repeat with the remaining batter until all the pancakes are cooked, using more butter or oil to grease the pan between each batch. Serve plain or top with a bit of maple sugar or syrup.

⅓ cup (27 g) coarsely ground coffee

4 tablespoons (8 g) loose leaf chai, or 4 bags of chai

1½ cups (355 ml) boiling hot water

1½ cups (355 ml) milk

2 tablespoons (40 g) maple syrup, or more or less to taste

A camping French press

FRENCH PRESS DIRTY CHAI

YIELD: 2 servings

What is a dirty chai latte, you ask? It is a chai latte laced with a shot of espresso. Warm and soothing milk steeped with exotic spicy fragrance that wafts enticingly into your face. It's like the beverage version of a rejuvenating back rub and aromatherapy . . . or something. The perfect antidote to too much running around. And, it can be yours while you relax by a fire midmorning, or midday, or mid nothing at all, if you just have a French press and the right ingredients.

---

1. Put the ground coffee and the tea in the bottom of your French press. (If using tea bags, open them and empty the tea into the French press. You'll likely wind up with tea dust in your drink since bag tea is finer, but that's okay.) Pour the hot water in, allow to steep for about 7 minutes, and then press.

2. While the coffee and tea are steeping, gently warm your milk.

3. Divide the coffee-tea mixture into 2 mugs, add 1 tablespoon (20 g) of maple syrup to each mug, and stir to dissolve. Pour warm milk into each mug. Enjoy!

2

QUICK LUNCHES

Curried Tuna Salad 34
Summer Sausage Sandwich 37
Farmer's Lunch Sandwich 38
Smoked Salmon and Bagel Sandwich 41
Turkey and Guacamole Wrap 42
Almond Butter Wrap with Dried Fruit and Cinnamon 45
Chickpea Salad with Pita 46

CURRIED TUNA SALAD

YIELD: 4 servings

There's something transformative about the combination of curry powder and tuna—it's unexpected (versus chicken salad, for example, where you kind of do expect it) but familiar at the same time. And it's straight-up good.

2 cans or pouches of tuna (drained, if cans)

¼ cup (60 g) mayonnaise

2 teaspoons (4 g) curry powder

Squeeze of lemon juice

2 tablespoons (18 g) golden raisins

1. Stir together the tuna, mayonnaise, curry powder, and lemon juice until well mixed. Then stir in the raisins.

2. Serve on ciabatta with very ripe tomato slices and arugula. Serve as an open-faced sandwich on a slice of bread with avocado. Serve on celery sticks. Serve on nori sheets.

TIP

All of the standard varieties of canned tuna—white or light, oil-packed or water-packed—work fine in this recipe. Our favorite? White tuna packed in water.

2 slices of your favorite sturdy, packable bread

2 to 3 ounces (57–85 g) of a packable hard sliced cheese, like cheddar

2 ounces (55 g) sliced summer sausage

SUMMER SAUSAGE SANDWICH

YIELD: 1 serving

Other than peanut butter and jelly, this might be the best sandwich for camping. Summer sausages are ones that don't need to be refrigerated, making this an easy spur-of-the-moment on-the-trail lunch.

Layer the cheese and sausage on 1 slice of bread and top with the other. If you've brought mayo and mustard packets, smear your bread with those as well. That's it!

TIP

Feeling fancy? Upscale this sandwich with authentic Italian coppa, capicola, or prosciutto in place of the summer sausage, and serve on a sliced ciabatta roll instead of sandwich bread.

FARMER'S LUNCH SANDWICH

YIELD: 1 sandwich

The simplicity of the Farmer's Lunch sandwich is deceiving—it tastes like *so* much more than the sum of its parts. The sharp cheese, the sweet-tart apple, and the brine of the pickles with the mayo and mustard all thrum together like a symphony.

¼ of a nice, crusty baguette, sliced in half horizontally

1 tablespoon (14 g) good mayonnaise

1 tablespoon (11 g) grainy mustard

3 to 4 ounces (85 to 115 g) really sharp cheddar cheese, sliced

¼ tart apple (such as Granny Smith), cut into thin slices

5 to 6 slices of bread and butter pickle (or pickled green tomatoes if you can get them)

1 large leaf of lettuce (optional)

1. Smear each side of the baguette with half the mayo and half the mustard.

2. On the bottom half of the baguette, layer on the cheese, apple slices, and pickle slices, then add the lettuce if using.

3. Cover with the top half of the baguette. Enjoy!

TIP

You need a sweeter pickle for this sandwich. A standard dill pickle makes it too tart, too sour. Sliced sweet gherkins are a good alternative for the bread and butter pickles, if you happen to be a gherkin fan.

1 bagel, sliced in half (if you want it toasted, you will have to toast it in a pan or over the fire ahead of time)

1 to 2 ounces (28 to 55 g) cream cheese

1 tablespoon (6 g) sliced scallions

1 to 2 ounces (28 to 55 g) hot smoked salmon (the kind that is flaky and opaque, not the translucent soft kind that is cold smoked salmon or lox)

Lettuce and sliced tomato (optional but yummy)

SMOKED SALMON AND BAGEL SANDWICH

YIELD: 1 sandwich

Salmon and cream cheese bagels are not just for eating as you walk from your subway stop to work in New York City. In fact, this salmon bagel is an entirely different beast with hot smoked salmon instead of lox and scallions instead of red onions and capers. But, like its big-city counterpart, it is delicious and surprisingly amenable to being a meal on the go.

1. Spread cream cheese on both halves of the bagel.

2. Sprinkle half the scallion slices on each bagel half and press them into the cream cheese.

3. Layer the smoked salmon (and lettuce and tomato, if using) on the bottom half of the bagel. Cover with the other half and enjoy.

TURKEY AND GUACAMOLE WRAP

YIELD: 1 wrap

This may sound like just another turkey and guacamole wrap . . . But it is a turkey and guacamole wrap with *pizzazz*! The extra oomph comes from a hefty dose of mayonnaise and black pepper. And while using both mayonnaise *and* guacamole may seem like a little much in the condiment department, it's worth it. The spice, tang, and creaminess give deli turkey new life. Plus you're camping, so you deserve it.

1 large tortilla

2 tablespoons (28 g) mayonnaise

A generous sprinkling of ground black pepper

3 tablespoons (42 g) guacamole

About ¼ pound (115 g) shaved or sliced turkey breast

2 to 3 slices of ripe tomato

A small handful of arugula leaves (or other lettuce, but arugula's peppery flavor is nice here)

1. Spread the mayonnaise on the tortilla, then sprinkle it with a generous amount of black pepper. Spread on the guacamole, then top with the turkey. Add the tomato slices and arugula.

2. Fold the bottom and top in, then roll up the wrap like a burrito. Wrap tightly in parchment or wax paper or place in an airtight sandwich container to transport. Or eat it right away!

TIP

If there is no guacamole on hand, simply add some slices of avocado and tomato drizzled with lime juice and sprinkled with salt.

GERBER

1 flour tortilla

1 to 2 tablespoons (16 to 32 g) salted almond butter (if you have unsalted almond butter, sprinkle a nice pinch of salt over yours after spreading)

1 to 2 tablespoons (15 to 30 g) of your choice of dried fruit

A pinch of cinnamon

ALMOND BUTTER WRAP WITH DRIED FRUIT AND CINNAMON

YIELD: 1 serving

Maybe you noticed right away, maybe you didn't, but this is just a glorified peanut butter and jelly wrap. It takes the most stalwart of all trail lunches and gives it a wee twist, swapping peanut butter for almond butter and messy jelly for tidily packaged dried fruit. Then it makes it all fragrant and fancy with a pinch of cinnamon.

This will work with any nut butter, or even with tahini (adding a pinch or two of salt is a must!) or sunflower seed butter.

Spread the almond butter on the tortilla, and sprinkle over dried fruit and a pinch of cinnamon. Roll up and enjoy.

TIP

Dried fruits such as apples, apricots, dates, figs, peaches, and prunes will taste good in this sandwich.

CHICKPEA SALAD WITH PITA

YIELD: 2 to 4 servings

It's the flavors of a falafel wrap with tahini sauce turned into a salad! This light yet nutrient-packed meal will fuel you for hours of camping.

1 large garnet yam, peeled and cut into 1-inch (2.5 cm) cubes

Olive oil

Salt

1 15-ounce (425 g) can chickpeas, drained and rinsed

2 garlic cloves, peeled

1 tablespoon (40 g) chopped red onion

1 tablespoon (15 g) tahini

1 teaspoon ground cumin

¼ cup (60 ml) fresh lemon juice

½ cup (30 g) chopped fresh parsley

FOR SERVING

Cucumber slices

Cherry tomatoes, halved

Pitas or another soft flatbread

---

1. Heat your oven to 425°F (220°C, or gas mark 7). Toss the cubed yam with about 1 tablespoon (15 ml) of olive oil and sprinkle it with salt. Spread on a baking sheet and roast, stirring occasionally until cooked through and browned on the outside, about 40 minutes.

2. In a frying pan over medium heat, add about 1 tablespoon (15 ml) of olive oil and heat until shimmering. Add the chickpeas and the whole garlic cloves. Cook, stirring, until the garlic is golden on the outside and the chickpeas are warmed, about 3 to 4 minutes. Remove from heat.

3. Finely chop the 2 sautéed garlic cloves. In a large bowl, whisk together the garlic, red onion, tahini, cumin, 1 tablespoon (15 ml) of olive oil, lemon juice, and a generous pinch of salt. Whisk a spoonful of water into the dressing if you need to increase its creaminess and make it thinner. Add the cooked yam, chickpeas, and parsley and toss to coat everything with the dressing. Taste and add more salt, if desired. Allow to cool to room temperature, then transfer to an airtight container.

4. Serve the chickpea salad scooped into pita breads along with slices of cucumber and cherry tomato halves.

3

TRAIL SNACKS

Granola Bars 50
Camper's Cookies 53
Maple-Blueberry Fruit Leather 54
Trail Mix #1: Twist on Traditional 57
Trail Mix #2: Kinda Fancy 58
Trail Mix #3: Chunky Monkey 61

GRANOLA BARS

YIELD: 10 bars

If you ever look at your grocery receipts and notice just how much money you spend on organic granola bars for your three-year-old who consumes them like they are the base of the food pyramid, suddenly making your own granola bars seems like a reasonable and frugal activity. Plus they taste better than the store-bought kind, and they pack quite well. Throw a container in your backpack to prevent midhike meltdowns. Can't do nuts? Tahini or sunflower seed butter will also work well in these granola bars.

1¼ cups (125 g) rolled oats

⅓ cup (46 g) whole wheat flour (replace with ground flaxseed for a gluten-free bar)

3 tablespoons (27 g) cornmeal

1 cup (175 g) finely chopped pitted dates

1 teaspoon salt

½ teaspoon ground cinnamon

⅓ cup (115 g) honey

¼ cup (60 ml) olive oil

¼ cup (65 g) creamy peanut butter

½ teaspoon lemon zest

---

1. Preheat the oven to 350°F (180°C, or gas mark 4). Line an 8" × 8" (20 × 20 cm) baking pan with parchment paper. (Aluminum foil will also work.)

2. In one bowl, combine the oats, whole wheat flour, cornmeal, dates, salt, and cinnamon. In a separate bowl, whisk together the honey, olive oil, peanut butter, and lemon zest. Scrape the wet ingredients into the bowl of the dry ingredients and stir well until everything is completely coated.

3. Dump the mixture into the prepared pan and pat it into an even layer with your fingers (there's enough olive oil that it won't stick to your fingers). Bake for 20 to 25 minutes or until well browned around the edges but still soft in the center. Cool the bars to room temperature, then use a sharp knife to cut into 10 pieces, about 4" × 1½" (10 × 4 cm). Stack the bars in a sealed, airtight container with parchment paper between the layers and allow them to chill in the fridge for at least another 30 minutes to fully set them. Store and transport in the airtight container.

2⅓ cups (292 g) all-purpose flour

1 teaspoon baking soda

1 teaspoon ground cinnamon

¾ teaspoon salt

2 cups (180 g) rolled oats (old-fashioned oats, not quick cooking)

½ cup (42 g) shredded coconut

½ cup (50 g) roughly chopped pecans

1 cup (145 g) raisins

1 cup (203 g) candy-coated chocolate pieces (like M&Ms)

1 cup (224 g) unsalted butter, softened to room temperature

1½ cups (360 g) light brown sugar

½ cup (100 g) granulated sugar

2 large eggs and 1 egg yolk, at room temperature

1 teaspoon vanilla extract

CAMPER'S COOKIES

YIELD: 2 dozen cookies

These are a classic take on cowboy cookies, which are basically a spin-off of oatmeal cookies. These cookies are sturdy for packing, buttery for eating, and contain every snacky niblet you could possibly want.

1. Preheat the oven to 350°F (180°C, or gas mark 4). In a large bowl, combine all the dry ingredients—flour, baking soda, cinnamon, salt, oats, coconut, pecans, raisins, and chocolate pieces—and stir together to combine.

2. In the bowl of a stand mixer fitted with a paddle attachment, blend together the butter and sugars until fluffy (you can also use a handheld mixer). Add the eggs and yolk 1 at a time, followed by the vanilla, continuing to beat on a medium-low speed until well combined and smooth.

3. Fold the dry ingredients into the wet ingredients using a rubber spatula or wooden spoon, mixing until just combined.

4. Scoop 2-inch (5 cm) balls of dough onto baking sheets (line the baking sheets with parchment paper for easier cleanup, if you'd like), leaving about 2 inches (5 cm) between each cookie for room to spread. Refrigerate the dough balls for about 20 minutes before baking. (This is not absolutely required but definitely recommended.)

5. Bake 1 sheet at a time until the edges of the cookies are brown and set but the centers of the cookies are still just a bit soft, about 12 to 14 minutes. Allow the cookies to set by cooling them on the sheets for a few minutes before transferring them to a wire rack to cool completely. These cookies store well in an airtight container and can be packed into a zip-top plastic bag for hikes and outings.

MAPLE-BLUEBERRY FRUIT LEATHER

YIELD: About 18 pieces

This blueberry-maple fruit leather is chewy and snackable with a flavor reminiscent of blueberry pie filling. Dehydrating fruit leather takes a while, but this snack is worth the time.

4 cups (580 g) fresh or frozen and defrosted blueberries

¼ cup (80 g) pure maple syrup

1 tablespoon (15 ml) lemon juice

1 teaspoon vanilla extract

SPECIAL EQUIPMENT

Blender

Food dehydrator

1. Combine the blueberries, maple syrup, lemon juice, and vanilla extract in a blender and blend until smooth.

2. If you want particularly smooth fruit leather, more like what you would get commercially, you can strain the fruit puree through a fine mesh strainer to remove any chunks.

3. Line your dehydrator trays with parchment paper or the silicone baking mats they make for dehydrators, then spread the fruit mixture into the trays. Spread each layer out evenly about ⅛ inch (3 mm) thick with a spatula, making the edges a little thicker than the rest. This ensures full drying.

4. Set your dehydrator to 135°F (57°C) and dehydrate your fruit leather until it is, well, leathery. It should take about 6 to 8 hours, but times may vary. It should be pliable and nonsticky to the touch. When they are done, allow them to cool fully before taking them off the trays. Slice the fruit leathers into your desired sizes of rectangle and roll each up with parchment paper. Store in an airtight container in a cool, dark place for up to 2 weeks.

1 cup (100 g) raw pecans

½ cup (65 g) raw almonds (or other nut)

1 tablespoon (15 ml) olive oil

Pinch of sea salt

½ cup (60 g) dried cranberries

½ cup (80 g) golden raisins

½ cup (87 g) dark chocolate chips

TRAIL MIX #1: TWIST ON TRADITIONAL

YIELD: 3 cups (450 g)

There's a reason GORP stands for "good old raisins and peanuts." The combination is classic, timeless, and tasty. BUT it's even better with pecans. When pecans are toasted, they are a most superior nut, roasted and sweet and complex. Because they are kind of a fancy nut, stretch them here by adding some other bulky nut of your choice. Other than that, this trail mix hews pretty close to the traditional, aside from combining raisins with dried cranberries for an extra sweet-tart pop.

Change it up: If you're a fan of the cashew-Craisin mixes that are popular in the grocery snack aisle these days, you can take a cue from them. Use cashews instead of pecans and white chocolate chips instead of dark chocolate.

1. Preheat the oven to 300°F (150°C, or gas mark 2). Toss the pecans and almonds with the olive oil and a hefty pinch of sea salt and spread onto a baking sheet. Bake in the oven, stirring occasionally, until toasted but not deep brown, approximately 10 minutes. Allow to completely cool to room temperature.

2. Mix the nuts, dried fruit, and chocolate chips together in a large bowl, and then divide into sealable bags.

TRAIL MIX #2: KINDA FANCY

YIELD: 6 cups (1015 g)

This recipes makes a fun trail mix alternative. Fiery crunchy wasabi peas, savory sesame sticks, and bits of nori take cheesy Goldfish in an unexpectedly tasty direction.

4 cups (804 g) cheesy Goldfish crackers (you could use other cheese crackers, but then you wouldn't get to think about how funny it is to have fish and seaweed together in your snack mix)

1 cup (120 g) sesame sticks

1 cup (91 g) wasabi peas

1 sheet nori, cut into short, thin strips, kind of like seaweed confetti

Stir all of the ingredients together and transfer them into a tightly sealed container—that's it!

TIP

If you will have children along when you camp, let them taste the wasabi peas before you make this mix. If the kids say the peas are too spicy, substitute roasted salted green peas, which are available in most supermarkets, often in the healthy snacks section.

1 cup (100 g) halved walnuts

½ tablespoon (8 ml) olive oil

Pinch of sea salt

3 cups (100 g) peanut butter–filled pretzels

1 cup (175 g) dark chocolate chips or chocolate chunks

1 cup (127 g) dried banana chips

TRAIL MIX #3: CHUNKY MONKEY

YIELD: 6 cups (1015 g)

This trail mix makes a great emergency snack when hunger has tipped over the thin edge from vaguely uncomfortable to anger inducing.

1. Preheat the oven to 300°F (150°C, or gas mark 2). Toss the walnuts with olive oil and a pinch of sea salt and spread on a baking sheet. Bake until toasted and fragrant, about 10 minutes. Allow to completely cool to room temperature.

2. Mix all the ingredients in a large bowl, and then divide into sealable bags.

TIP

Raisins, craisins, and dried apples can be substituted for (or added to) the dried banana chips in this recipe.

4

MAIN COURSES

Grilled Bread with Toppings 64
Pita or Naan Pizzas 67
Paella with Chorizo 68
Campfire Irish Stew 71
Forest Leczó (Hungarian Stew) 72
Pie Iron Chimichangas 75
Campfire Nachos 76
Perfect T-Bone Steak 78
Pineapple Pork 80
Sticky Pork Belly 83
Lamb Chops with Pomegranate Sauce 84
Grilled Chicken Fajita Kebabs 87
Pie Iron Chicken Potpies 88
Chicken from Hell 91
Fish Curry 92
Cod Wrapped in Bacon 95
Herb-Crusted Cod 96

GRILLED BREAD WITH TOPPINGS

YIELD: 8 servings

Bread drizzled with olive oil, dusted with salt, and licked with flame is so simple, yet it is one of the most magical-tasting things. Surpassing human comprehension to understand what makes it so good, it may just be that it is what peace tastes like. One way or another, you should probably share this peace with others. Simply grill bread over the fire for your crew and set out a variety of toppings.

About 16 slices of rustic, crusty bread like a ciabatta or sourdough (use small pieces if this is a snack/appetizer and large slices if this is the star of the show)

Olive oil

Salt

TOPPINGS BUFFET

2 cups (500 g) whole-milk ricotta

2 ripe avocados, peeled, pitted, and smashed

About 3 ounces (85 g) prosciutto, coppa, or other salty cured meat

3 to 4 ounces (85 to 115 g) smoked trout or salmon, broken into bits

½ cup (75 g) cherry tomatoes, halved

½ hothouse cucumber, cut into slices

Apricot jam

Flaky sea salt for sprinkling

Chile flakes for sprinkling

Honey for drizzling

Chopped herbs, if desired

1. Brush each slice of bread on both sides with olive oil and sprinkle lightly with salt. Grill the bread slices on both sides over medium-hot coals until they are toasted and show light char lines, about 2 minutes per side.

2. Pile the grilled bread on a serving tray and set out the buffet of toppings. Let people pile things onto their bread in their desired combinations.

TIP

We call for cherry tomatoes in this recipe because they tend to taste good year-round. If it is mid- to late-summer and full-sized tomatoes are at their peak freshness, by all means slice them up and use them instead of cherry tomatoes.

4 store-bought pitas or naan breads

1 24-ounce (735 g) jar tomato sauce

TOPPINGS

Pepperoni

Canned pineapple pieces

Shredded mozzarella

A few wheels of very thinly sliced lemon, peel on

Prosciutto

Sliced green olives

Fresh mozzarella

Fresh basil

Olive oil

PITA OR NAAN PIZZAS

YIELD: 4 individual pizzas

Grilling pizza with fresh dough can be super fun if you're up for it. But, it can also be stressful and fiddly, with dough tearing and drooping and charring while toddlers run away because dinner is taking too long. For the days, and especially on trips, where you want pizza on the menu but you want to keep it really simple, take a classic shortcut and using prepared pita bread or naan breads for crusts. You still get the fun of everyone choosing their toppings and the deliciousness of fresh hot pizza but without having to worry about nailing the crust.

1. Place a cast-iron skillet (or another heavy skillet) on a grill over medium heat. Let the skillet get warm.

2. For each pizza, place a pita or naan into the skillet and let the first side toast for 1 minute. Flip, then quickly add the tomato sauce and toppings and cover the pan. Allow the pizza to cook until the cheese is melted, then transfer to a plate. Repeat the process with each of the remaining pitas/naans until everyone has a pizza.

PIZZA TOPPING COMBO 1

Pizza sauce, pepperoni, canned pineapple chunks, olive slices, and shredded mozzarella. Sprinkle on fresh basil after the pizza is cooked.

PIZZA TOPPING COMBO 2

Thinly sliced pieces of lemon, a little prosciutto, olive slices, slices of fresh mozzarella, and a drizzle of olive oil. Sprinkle on fresh basil after the pizza is cooked.

TIP

In general, don't go too overboard on the amount of pizza sauce or cheese, or it will be hard to get the cheese hot and melty without burning the bottom of the pizza.

PAELLA WITH CHORIZO

YIELD: 4 servings

Traditionally, chorizo isn't a part of paella, but it adds a great crunchiness once the chorizo is cooked and crisp. If you don't like it, leave it out next time. The best paella rice is a short-grain rice, such as bomba. If you can't find it, arborio makes a surprisingly good substitute, as does Calrose.

- 1⅔ cups (400 ml) chicken stock
- Large pinch of saffron threads
- 5⅓ ounces (150 g) smoked chorizo, very thinly sliced
- 2 chicken breasts, cut into 1-inch (2.5 cm) pieces
- 2 tablespoons (30 ml) olive oil
- 1 yellow onion, diced
- 3 garlic cloves, sliced
- 1 red bell pepper, diced
- 1 teaspoon smoked paprika
- 12½ ounces (350 g) paella rice
- 2 tomatoes, diced
- ⅓ cup (50 g) fresh peas, or scant ½ cup (50 g) frozen and thawed
- 6 medium or large shrimp, peeled and deveined
- 1 lemon, cut into wedges
- Chopped fresh parsley for garnish

1. Prepare your fire for medium heat.

2. Pour the stock into your camp cup and place it near the campfire (or pour it into a small saucepan and place it on the grill). Add the saffron threads.

3. In a large cast-iron skillet over medium heat, cook the chorizo until golden and curled on both sides. Remove the chorizo from the skillet and add the chicken to the fat that remained behind. Cook until browned on all sides (it doesn't have to be cooked through at this point). Remove from the skillet.

4. Pour the oil into the skillet and heat until hot. Add the onion and garlic and cook, stirring frequently, until browned and the vegetables start to soften. Stir in the bell pepper and cook for 2 minutes more. Stir in the paprika until everything is well coated. Add the rice and cook, stirring, until lightly toasted, about 1 minute. Add the warmed stock and bring the mixture to a boil.

5. Add the chicken and tomatoes. Stir to evenly distribute the ingredients, cover with an inverted skillet (or close the grill lid), and cook until the rice is tender and most of the stock is absorbed, 15 to 20 minutes.

6. Stir in the chorizo and peas, taking care not to disturb the rice on the bottom of the skillet. Dot the top with the shrimp, re-cover the skillet, and cook until the stock is fully absorbed and the shrimp is cooked through, just a few minutes. Remove from the heat.

7. Garnish with a squeeze of lemon juice and parsley before digging in.

About 14 ounces (400 g) boneless lamb steaks (thin-cut), cut into 1-inch (2.5 cm) pieces

3 garlic cloves, sliced

¾ cup plus 1 tablespoon plus 1 teaspoon (200 ml) beef broth

3 celery stalks, sliced ¼- to ½-inch (0.6 to 1 cm) thick

1 white or yellow onion, coarsely chopped

1 large carrot, sliced into ¼- to ½-inch (0.6 to 1 cm) coins

1 cup (240 ml) red wine

1 cup (240 ml) Guinness

4 dried bay leaves

6 whole allspice berries

1 tablespoon (1 g) dried parsley

1 teaspoon table salt

1 teaspoon ground black pepper

2 medium potatoes, peeled and chopped into ½- to 1-inch (1 to 2.5 cm) pieces

Chopped fresh parsley for garnish

CAMPFIRE IRISH STEW

YIELD: 4 servings

Imagine gathering around a crackling fire with a warm bowl of hearty stew in hand. This the perfect meal for one of those colder days out in the forest, bringing the comforting flavors of Ireland to your campsite.

1. Prepare your fire for medium heat.

2. Place a large well-seasoned pot over medium heat. Add the lamb and cook until browned. Add the garlic and cook for 1 minute, pour in the broth, and bring it to a boil. Stir in the celery, onion, and carrot.

3. Carefully add the wine, Guinness, bay leaves, and spices. Cover the pot and cook until the lamb and vegetables are tender, 30 to 40 minutes.

4. Add the potatoes, re-cover the pot, and cook until tender, 15 to 20 minutes more. Serve, sprinkled with chopped fresh parsley.

FOREST LECZÓ (HUNGARIAN STEW)

YIELD: 4 servings

Although this stew has Hungarian roots, different Eastern European countries put their own spins on it. The sunny-side-up egg adds a pop of color, but feel free to skip it.

About 11 ounces (300 g) smoked pork belly, skin removed, chopped

1 (5⅓-ounce [150 g]) Polish sausage (smoked kielbasa), diced

1 yellow onion, finely diced

4 garlic cloves, sliced

3 bell peppers (a mix of colors), cut into strips

2 large tomatoes, diced

1 medium zucchini, diced

1⅔ cups (400 g) tomato sauce

1 teaspoon dried marjoram, plus more as needed

1 teaspoon paprika, plus more as needed

1 teaspoon table salt, plus more as needed

1 teaspoon ground black pepper, plus more as needed

3 or 4 dried bay leaves

4 large eggs (optional)

Chopped fresh parsley for garnish

---

1. Prepare your fire for medium-high heat.

2. In a large pot over medium-high heat, combine the pork belly and sausage. Cook until they start to brown and render their fat, then add the onion and garlic and cook until softened and brown. You can lower the heat to medium at this point.

3. Add the vegetables, tomato sauce, spices, and bay leaves. Stir well and let the mixture bubble away until the vegetables are very soft and the stew is thick, 1 to 1½ hours. Taste for seasoning and remove from the heat. Remove and discard the bay leaves.

4. If using the eggs, place a large cast-iron skillet over medium heat and fry them to your liking, seasoned with salt and pepper. Top each bowl of stew with 1 egg and sprinkle with parsley.

PIE IRON CHIMICHANGAS

YIELD: 4 servings

What is a chimichanga, you ask? It is basically a fried burrito. Of course, deep-frying is quite an undertaking. Toasting your chimichanga in the fire, on the other hand, is . . . still a bit of an undertaking, given you need to make a fire and all. But still way less intimidating somehow. You could make these with any favorite taco meat and beans, but ground beef and refried beans seem like the coziest and most comforting.

- 4 10-inch (25 cm) flour tortillas
- 1 pound (455 g) of your favorite taco beef, precooked at home
- 1 16-ounce (454 g) can refried beans
- 1 cup (115 g) shredded mild cheddar cheese
- Cooking spray oil
- Sour cream and salsa for serving

1. Lay out a tortilla. Toward one side of the tortilla, place a heaping scoop of beef, a scoop of refried beans, and a sprinkling of cheese in a line, leaving space at the top and bottom of the tortilla. Then fold the side nearest the fillings over the fillings to cover them. Fold in the top and bottom and then continue to roll up the tortilla like a burrito.

2. Spray a pie iron well with cooking spray, then put the chimichanga in it. Cook over the fire or in the coals, flipping occasionally, until the tortilla is browned and the filling is warmed through, about 5 to 8 minutes, depending on your fire. Remove from the fire, carefully unlatch, and check the cooking progress as often as you'd like.

3. Repeat to cook all the chimichangas. Serve them warm with sour cream and salsa. (And any other toppings you like!)

CAMPFIRE NACHOS

YIELD: 4 servings

Whether you make a dinner of nachos or want to make some for lunch or a predinner snack, this is less a recipe per se and more an FYI: You can make nachos in a foil pack over a grill! Or on a grate over your campfire!

1. Lay out 2 sheets of aluminum foil that are each about 12" x 24" (30 x 60 cm). On each sheet, lay down a cup (26 g) of chips in a single layer, then sprinkle one quarter of the cheese over the top. If you are using any of the other nice-to-have things, sprinkle some on the layer as well. Add another layer of chips to each foil pack, sprinkle with the remainder of the cheese (and other toppings), then top with the remainder of the chips. Having chips on both the top and bottom helps prevent some of the cheese from getting stuck to the foil, although collateral cheese loss is just kind of part of the life of nachos.

2. Fold the foil packets over and roll the edges tightly together to seal. Using a knife, punch a few small holes in the tops of your packets to allow steam to escape.

3. Place on a grill or grate over medium-high heat, and grill, turning occasionally, until the packet is warmed through and the cheese is melted. This generally takes anywhere from 6 to 15 minutes depending on how many toppings you are using. Serve with sour cream and salsa.

MUST HAVE

Aluminum foil

1 8-ounce (225 g) bag corn chips (about 6 or 7 cups [156 or 182 g] of chips)

2½ cups (283 g) shredded cheese, preferably a mix of mild cheddar and Jack cheese, but just one or the other works as well

Sour cream and salsa for serving

NICE TO HAVE

About 1 cup (225 g) precooked shredded pork or chicken

1 cup (256 g) canned black beans, drained and rinsed

1 large tomato, diced

Jalapeño slices

Canned black olives

Pickled red onions

PERFECT T-BONE STEAK

YIELD: Serves 2

This recipe uses a Polish potato seasoning called *przyprawa do ziemniaków*, a mixture of spices (such as caraway, coriander, dill, garlic, lemon zest, marjoram, onion, and paprika). It comes in a packet and is specifically for potatoes—similar to those packets for French onion soup mix or ranch dressing mix. Depending on where you are, you can find *przyprawa do ziemniaków* in stores, but, as always, use whatever spices you have or like on potatoes. The bit of lemon zest in this blend tastes nice; it breaks through the rich, fatty meat.

½ cup (1 stick) plus 2 tablespoons (150 g) butter, divided

2 medium potatoes, thinly sliced

2 tablespoons (30 ml) olive oil, divided

2 teaspoons potato seasoning (*przyprawa do ziemniaków*)

1 teaspoon table salt

1 teaspoon ground black pepper

9 garlic cloves, 5 sliced, 4 left whole

Handful of fresh parsley, finely chopped

Flaky sea salt

Freshly cracked black pepper

1 (1-inch [2.5 cm]-thick) T-bone steak

½ cup plus 2 tablespoons (150 ml) whiskey

Few thyme sprigs

Few rosemary sprigs

Cocktail tomatoes for presentation

1. Prepare your fire for high heat. (If using a grill, set up one side for high heat and one side for medium heat.)

2. Put half the butter in a camp cup and set it next to your fire while you gather your ingredients. (Or put it in a saucepan and set it on the medium-heat side of the grill.)

3. In a large bowl, toss the potatoes with 1 tablespoon (15 ml) oil, the potato seasoning, table salt, and ground pepper to coat.

4. To the melted butter, add the sliced garlic, parsley, a generous pinch of sea salt, and cracked pepper. Set aside.

5. Generously season the steak on all sides (including the edges!) with sea salt and cracked pepper, rubbing the spices in a bit.

6. Place a grill pan over high heat and pour in the remaining 1 tablespoon (15 ml) of oil. When smoking, add the steak, searing it on the fatty edge (you might have to hold it up) before setting it on its side and cooking until a deep golden crust and nice dark grill marks develop. Flip the steak and carefully pour the whiskey into the pan—it will likely ignite! (If you're using a gas grill, or this otherwise worries you, remove the pan from the flame before adding the whiskey, then return it to the heat.)

7. Let the whiskey burn off until the pan is almost dry, then add the remaining butter, along with the thyme, rosemary, and whole garlic. Cook, periodically basting the steak with the butter and juices, until done to your liking, 3 to 4 minutes per side. (Pay attention to the fillet because it will cook faster than the sirloin.) Transfer to a cutting board to rest while you cook the potatoes.

8. Prepare your fire for medium heat.

9. Add the potatoes and tomatoes to the skillet, cooking until the potatoes are crispy and have nice grill marks on both sides, 4 to 5 minutes.

10. Slice the steak, and spoon over the garlic-parsley butter. Serve a steak slice on a potato, with tomatoes for garnish.

PINEAPPLE PORK

YIELD: 2 or 3 servings

Sweet, tangy, and savory all at once, Pineapple Pork is a tropical-inspired dish that brings bold flavor with minimal effort.

1 (about 14-ounce [400 g]) pork tenderloin, trimmed

Table salt

Ground black pepper

2 tablespoons (30 g) butter or (30 ml) oil

5 or 6 (½-inch [0.6 cm]-thick) pineapple slices, halved

Large red bell pepper, finely chopped

2 fresh chiles (different colors, if desired), thinly sliced (seeds retained for more heat)

1 red onion, finely diced

1¼ cups (300 ml) pineapple juice

2½ tablespoons (50 g) honey

2 tablespoons (32 g) barbecue sauce

1 teaspoon paprika

1 teaspoon garlic powder

1 scallion, sliced

1. Prepare your fire for medium heat. (If using a grill, set up one side for medium heat and one side for low/indirect heat.)

2. Generously season all sides of the pork with salt and pepper.

3. In a large cast-iron skillet over medium heat, melt the butter. Add the pork to the skillet and sear all sides until deeply golden brown. Remove from the heat. Cut into the sides of the tenderloin, about 1 inch (2.5 cm) apart but not all the way through. Insert a pineapple slice into each cut (they will stick out of the top).

4. In a large bowl, stir together the bell pepper, chiles, onion, pineapple juice, honey, barbecue sauce, paprika, garlic powder, 1 teaspoon salt, and 1 teaspoon pepper.

5. Wipe out the skillet, return the pork to it, and place it over medium heat. Spoon a couple spoonfuls of the pepper sauce over the pork, then pour the rest of the sauce into the skillet. Bring to a boil, cover the skillet with an inverted skillet, and top with a large handful of coals, nearly covering the entire thing—this will lower the heat, which is fine, as you don't want a lot of heat from below. (If using a grill, move to low/indirect heat and close the grill lid.) Cook until the pork is cooked through to your liking and the sauce is thickened, 30 to 35 minutes, replenishing the coals as needed.

6. Remove the pork from the skillet and slice (we recommend down the middle). Spoon over more sauce and sprinkle with scallion before devouring.

4 garlic cloves, sliced

2-inch (5 cm) piece fresh ginger, peeled and finely diced

1 fresh red chile, finely diced (seeds retained for more heat)

½ teaspoon peppercorns

½ teaspoon flaky sea salt

6 tablespoons plus 2 teaspoons (100 ml) olive oil

2½ tablespoons (50 g) honey

3 tablespoons plus 1 teaspoon (50 ml) soy sauce

1 (2¼-pound, about 1 kg) slab pork belly cut into 1-inch (2.5 cm) cubes

1⅔ cups (400 ml) whiskey

Sesame seeds for garnish

Chopped fresh parsley or snipped fresh chives for garnish

STICKY PORK BELLY

YIELD: 4 to 6 servings

Pork belly and whiskey—together at last! Whiskey might not be a common ingredient in sticky pork belly, but the flavor blends well with the ginger and honey in the sauce.

1. Prepare your fire for medium-low heat.

2. Use a mortar and pestle to mash the garlic, ginger, chile, peppercorns, and salt into a paste. Pour in the oil, honey, and soy sauce and stir to combine. (If you don't have a mortar and pestle, combine the ingredients in a food processor and pulse a few times.) Set aside.

3. Place a large cast-iron skillet over medium-low heat. When hot, add the pork. Cook until browned on all sides and the fat starts to render. Carefully pour in the whiskey—it will likely ignite! (If you're using a gas grill, or this otherwise worries you, remove the skillet from the flame before adding the whiskey, then return it to the heat.) Continue to burn off the whiskey, then pour in the garlic-ginger sauce. Cook, uncovered, until the sauce is thick and glossy and the pork is cooked through, 1 to 1½ hours .

4. Serve garnished with sesame seeds and fresh parsley.

LAMB CHOPS WITH POMEGRANATE SAUCE

YIELD: 3 servings

The pomegranate sauce cuts through the richness of the lamb, elevating the dish with every bite. If lamb's not your thing, filet mignon would make an amazing substitute.

Table salt

2 medium potatoes, thickly sliced (½ inch [1 cm])

Ground black pepper

3 bone-in lamb chops

2 tablespoons (30 ml) olive oil, divided

4 thyme sprigs

¼ cup (½ stick [60 g]) butter

2 rosemary sprigs

1 pomegranate, arils removed

¾ cup plus 1 tablespoon plus 1 teaspoon (200 ml) red wine

1 teaspoon dried oregano

Paprika for seasoning

1. Prepare your fire for medium to high heat. (If using a grill, set up one side for high heat and one side for medium heat.)

2. Fill a large pot with 2 quarts (about 2 L) water, generously season the water with salt, and bring it to a boil over high heat. Add the potatoes and boil until tender, about 25 minutes. Meanwhile, prep the remaining ingredients.

3. Prepare your fire for medium heat.

4. Generously season the lamb chops on both sides with salt and pepper, pressing the spices into the meat.

5. Set a grill pan over medium heat and pour in 1 tablespoon (15 ml) oil. When shimmering, add the lamb chops and place a thyme sprig on top of each. Cook until a deeply golden crust forms, then flip. Add the butter and rosemary to the pan. Cook, periodically basting the lamb chops with the butter and juices, until done to your liking, 4 to 5 minutes per side. Transfer to a cutting board to rest, covering to keep warm, while you make the sauce and finish the potatoes. Clean the grill pan.

6. In a skillet over medium heat, combine the pomegranate arils, remaining thyme sprig, red wine, oregano, 1 teaspoon salt, and 1 teaspoon pepper. Cook until thickened and saucy, 15 to 20 minutes (the pom seeds are quite juicy!), then remove from the heat.

7. Return the clean grill pan to medium heat and pour in the remaining 1 tablespoon (15 ml) of oil. Drain the potatoes and place them in the grill pan. Sprinkle with salt, pepper, and paprika. Cook until golden grill marks develop, then flip and season the other side as you did the first, cooking until you have nice grill marks.

8. Serve the lamb, drizzled with the sauce, alongside the potatoes.

GRILLED CHICKEN FAJITA KEBABS

YIELD: 4 servings

Assembling chicken and vegetables onto skewers in advance at home makes it a breeze to get dinner onto the grill when you're out at a campfire. It really makes you look like you have your act together. These skewers take a page out of the fajita playbook, complementing the zippy marinated chicken with grilled onion and bell pepper.

FOR THE MARINADE

Juice of 1 lime

2 garlic cloves, minced

½ teaspoon salt

2 teaspoons chili powder

2 teaspoons ground cumin

FOR THE KEBABS

1 pound (455 g) boneless, skinless chicken thighs, cut into bite-size (¾-inch [1.9 cm]) chunks

1 red onion, cut into ¾-inch (1.9 cm) chunks

2 bell peppers in different colors, cut into ¾-inch (1.9 cm) chunks

1 to 2 tablespoons (15 to 30 ml) olive oil

Grilling skewers (bamboo skewers soaked 30 minutes in water, or metal skewers)

TO SERVE

Flour tortillas

Sour cream

Cilantro

Sliced avocado

Lime wedges

1. Whisk together the marinade ingredients, then place in a shallow dish and add the chicken pieces. Toss the chicken to coat. Cover the dish, place it in the refrigerator, and allow to marinate overnight.

2. After the meat has marinated, thread the chicken, onion, and bell pepper chunks on skewers in an alternating pattern. Place skewers in a heavy-duty zip-top bag or sealable container and pack in the coldest part of your cooler.

3. Brush the kebabs with olive oil. Place the skewers on a grill or grate over a campfire at medium-high heat. Grill, turning occasionally, until the vegetables are soft and the meat is cooked through to an internal temperature of 165°F (74°C), about 20 minutes.

4. Serve the kebabs with the tortillas and other toppings so everyone can assemble their own fajitas.

PIE IRON CHICKEN POTPIES

YIELD: 4 servings

Chicken potpie is one of those foods that sounds amazing in concept but rarely is in fact. Not so when you turn it into a sandwich. Suddenly it is tidy, contained, and even more supremely satisfying. You may have seen pie iron potpies that are a quick combination of precooked chicken and a can of condensed soup. Not this version. For optimal deliciousness, make your filling mostly from scratch, although rotisserie chicken is one nice shortcut. It's worth it. Prep the filling at home, bring it to your fire, and be rewarded with tender, richly flavored, vegetable-studded individual potpie delights.

FOR THE FILLING

1 small rotisserie chicken

2 tablespoons (28 g) butter

1 yellow onion, peeled and chopped

3 garlic cloves, peeled and sliced

2 celery stalks, thinly sliced

1 large carrot, diced

½ cup (65 g) frozen peas

¼ teaspoon dried thyme

2 tablespoons (16 g) flour

1 cup (235 ml) dry white wine

1 cup (237 ml) heavy cream

FOR COOKING

8 slices of enriched bread such as brioche or challah (You can also use 8 biscuits from a tube, pressed out into thin squares, if you wish! This will increase the cooking time to about 12 minutes.)

Cooking spray oil

---

1. Peel the skin off the rotisserie chicken, pull the meat off the bones, and cut or tear into small pieces. Set aside. (Freeze the bones and skin for making stock at some future date, if you wish.)

2. In a large skillet, heat the butter until it melts and foams. Stir in the onion and cook until it starts to soften and get translucent, about 3 minutes. Add the garlic, celery, and carrots and cook, stirring frequently, until the garlic is golden and the celery and carrot have started to get tender, about 5 to 8 minutes, then stir in the peas.

3. Sprinkle the thyme and flour over the vegetables and stir to coat. Cook for about 2 to 3 minutes to get the raw flavor out of the flour, then add the wine, stirring vigorously to smooth out any lumps. Cook for about 2 minutes to cook off the alcohol, then stir in the cream. Bring to a light simmer and fold in the chicken.

4. The mixture should be quite thick because we are putting it into sandwiches instead of baking it in a potpie. If it seems soupy at all, continue to gently cook it until it is gloopy, for lack of a better word. Then, remove from the heat, cover, and cool. Transfer to an airtight container and refrigerate until you're heading to your fire.

5. Spray your pie iron on both sides with cooking spray. Place 1 piece of bread in it, spoon a couple of large spoonfuls of chicken filling in the middle, and then top with another piece of bread. Latch the pie iron and cook in the fire over medium-low coals until the outside is toasted brown and the inside is heated through, about 5 to 8 minutes.

6. Repeat to cook the remaining pies.

6 jalapeño peppers

3½ ounces (100 g) fresh mozzarella cheese, sliced into small planks or sticks

1 small yellow onion, finely diced

5 fresh chiles, sliced (seeds retained for more heat)

4 garlic cloves, thinly sliced

2½ tablespoons (50 g) honey

1 lemon, thinly cut into 6 slices (reserve the remaining lemon)

1 (12-ounce [355 ml]) bottle beer

3 chicken breasts, butterflied (do not cut all the way through)

Flaky sea salt

Freshly cracked black pepper

Sweet paprika for seasoning

1 to 2 tablespoons (15 to 30 ml) oil

Chopped fresh parsley for garnish

CHICKEN FROM HELL

YIELD: 3 servings

There's a reason this is called chicken from hell: It's fiery hot! You can use whatever fresh chiles you enjoy or have on hand. You can also choose which jalapeño variety to use; orange jalapeños add major spice while larger sweet mini peppers tame the heat.

1. Prepare your fire for medium heat.

2. Slice the jalapeños down one side, below the stem, taking care not to cut all the way through the peppers. Stuff each with mozzarella slices. Set aside.

3. In a small bowl, stir together the onion, fresh chiles, garlic, honey, juice from the remaining unsliced lemon, and beer.

4. Generously season the chicken on both sides with sea salt, cracked pepper, and paprika.

5. Place a large cast-iron skillet over medium heat and pour in the oil. When shimmering, add the chicken to the skillet. Cook until deeply golden brown and gorgeous, then flip. Cook for a couple minutes to sear, then add the beer mixture and bring it to a steady boil.

6. Nestle in the poppers, cheese-side up. Top the chicken with the lemon slices, then cover the skillet with an inverted skillet (or close the grill lid). Top with a large handful of coals, covering nearly the whole skillet, and cook until the chicken is done and the sauce is thickened, 20 to 25 minutes. You want this to cook slowly, so it's okay if the fire dies down as you replenish the coals on top.

7. Serve, sprinkled with parsley, along with the pan sauce and the poppers.

FISH CURRY

YIELD: 2 servings

For this curry, choose any white fish you like—barramundi, haddock, halibut, pollock, even salmon can stand up to these flavors and this heat.

1 cup (200 g) short-grain white rice

Table salt

2 tablespoons (30 ml) oil

1 red onion, finely diced

4 garlic cloves, thinly sliced

1- to 2-inch (2.5 to 5 cm) piece fresh ginger, peeled and finely chopped

2 tomatoes, 1 diced, 1 quartered

3 tablespoons (19 g) curry powder

1 tablespoon (5.6 g) red pepper flakes

1 tablespoon (7 g) ground cumin

1 tablespoon (6.8 g) ground turmeric

1. Prepare your fire for medium heat.

2. In a large cast-iron pot, combine the rice and a good pinch of salt. Pour in enough water to cover the rice by ¾ inch (1.5 cm). Cover the pot with a tight-fitting lid and place it over medium heat. Cook until the water is absorbed, 15 to 20 minutes. Meanwhile, prepare the remaining ingredients.

3. In a large cast-iron skillet over medium heat, heat the oil until shimmering. Add the onion, garlic, and ginger. Cook until softened and caramelized. Stir in the diced tomato, spices, and 1 teaspoon salt. Cook until the tomato is broken down, just a few minutes, then pour in the stock and stir in the tomato paste. Bring the mixture to a boil and add the chiles, bell peppers, and quartered tomato. Cook until the tomato and peppers are softened, a few minutes, then add the coconut milk, stirring until well blended. Add the fish and simmer until cooked through, 5 to 7 minutes.

4. Spoon the curry over the rice. Squeeze over a wedge of lime and add a sprinkle of fresh parsley.

¾ cup plus 1 tablespoon plus 1 teaspoon (200 ml) vegetable stock

2 tablespoons (32 g) tomato paste

3 fresh chiles, sliced (seeds retained for more heat)

2 bell peppers, any color, cut into strips

1 cup plus 2 teaspoons (250 ml) coconut milk

About 11 ounces (300 g) cod fillets, cut into 2-inch (5 cm) chunks

Lime wedges for seasoning

Chopped fresh parsley or cilantro for garnish

- ½ to 1 English cucumber, peeled and diced
- 1 small red onion, finely diced
- 1 tomato, diced
- 1 yellow bell pepper, diced
- ½ pineapple, peeled, cored, and diced
- Olive oil
- Table salt
- Ground black pepper
- Chopped fresh parsley for seasoning
- Bacon slices (about 22 slices)
- 2 (7-ounce [200 g]) skinless cod fillets
- Dried parsley for garnish
- ¾ cup plus 1 tablespoon plus 1 teaspoon (200 ml) white wine
- Lemon wedges for seasoning

COD WRAPPED IN BACON

YIELD: 2 servings

Everything tastes better with bacon, and cod is no exception. The fresh chopped salad on the side cuts through the richness and smokiness of that bacon, but use as much (or as little) of the salad ingredients as you like to round out your meal.

1. Prepare your fire for medium heat.

2. In a large bowl, combine the cucumber, onion, tomato, bell pepper, and pineapple. Drizzle with just enough oil to coat, but not pool, and toss to combine. Season with salt, pepper, and fresh parsley to taste. Taste for seasoning and set aside.

3. On a cutting board, lay down 5 bacon slices, just slightly overlapping each other. In the middle of these, place 2 bacon slices perpendicular to them. Lay 2 more perpendicular slices, going the other way, so you have a cross. Place a piece of fish in the middle (at the narrow ends on the 2 bacon slices), and generously season with salt, pepper, and dried parsley.

4. Wrap 2 bacon slices over the top of the fish, then do the same with the other 2 slices. Alternate wrapping the 5 bacon slices from either side. Repeat with the remaining fish, bacon, and spices.

5. Place a grill pan over medium heat and drizzle in 1 to 2 tablespoons (15 to 30 ml) of oil. Place the fish in the pan, bacon-ends-side down. Cook until golden brown and sizzling, then flip. Get a nice color to the bacon before adding the wine to the skillet. Continue cooking until the wine evaporates and the fish is cooked through, 10 to 15 minutes.

6. Slice the fish and spoon the salad over it and add a lemon wedge for squeezing.

HERB-CRUSTED COD

YIELD: 2 servings

The idea for this dish was to create pasta out of vegetables. You can cut the veggies into long, very thin strips, but by all means, use a spiralizer, if you have one. As for the fish, choose center-cut portions, for a nice square or rectangular slab. This ensures even cooking (and a better fit in the skillet).

Scant 1 cup (100 g) dried bread crumbs

Large handful of parsley, finely chopped, plus more for garnish

Handful of fresh basil, finely chopped

1 tablespoon (5.6 g) red pepper flakes

1 tablespoon plus 1 teaspoon (24 g) table salt

1 tablespoon plus 1 teaspoon (8 g) black pepper

2 large eggs, lightly beaten

¾ cup plus 1 heaping tablespoon (100 g) all-purpose flour

2 (6-ounce [170 g]) cod fillets

6 tablespoons plus 2 teaspoons (100 ml) oil, divided

3 tablespoons plus 1 teaspoon (50 g) butter

4 garlic cloves, minced

---

1. Prepare your fire for medium heat.

2. In a large bowl, combine the bread crumbs, parsley, basil, red pepper flakes, 1 tablespoon (18 g) salt, and 1 tablespoon (6 g) black pepper.

3. Set up a breading station with the eggs in a second bowl and the flour in a third bowl (or mounded on your cutting board).

4. Dredge each piece of fish in the flour, coating all sides, then dip it into the egg, allowing excess to drip off. Evenly coat the fish in the bread crumb mixture.

5. In a large cast-iron skillet over medium heat, combine 1 tablespoon (15 ml) oil and the butter. Add the garlic and cook until brown. Pour in the cream and stir in the mustard, lemon zest, lime zest, marjoram, remaining 1 teaspoon of salt, and remaining 1 teaspoon of pepper. Bring to a bubble and add the sliced vegetables. Cook until the vegetables are al dente, not more than 5 minutes, or the zucchini will disappear. Stir in the Parmesan and cook until melted and the flavors are blended. Remove the skillet from heat and transfer the vegetables to a platter or serving dish. Clean the skillet.

6. Return the clean skillet to medium heat and add the remaining 5 tablespoons plus 2 teaspoons (85 ml) of oil. When shimmering, add the coated fish and cook until a deep golden crust forms, about 3 minutes per side.

7. Spoon the veggie sauce over the fish and sprinkle with chopped parsley.

- ¾ cup plus 1 tablespoon plus 1 teaspoon (200 ml) heavy cream
- 2 tablespoons (30 g) whole-grain mustard
- Grated zest of 1 lemon
- Grated zest of 1 lime
- 1 tablespoon (1.7 g) dried marjoram
- 1 carrot, cut into thin "noodles"
- 1 parsnip, peeled and cut into thin "noodles"
- 1 red onion, sliced
- 1 medium zucchini, cut into thin "noodles"
- 1 scallion, sliced
- ½ cup (50 g) grated Parmesan cheese

5

FIRESIDE DESSERTS AND DRINKS

S'mores Revisited 100
Banana Boats 103
Campfire Bananas Foster 104
Foil-Pack Pears 107
Dutch Oven Apple Cake 108
Campfire Cobbler 111
Campfire Monkey Bread 112
Soft Chocolate Cookies 115
Flask Old-Fashioned 116
Apple Negroni 119
Shetland Sweater 120
Flask Red Rum 123

S'MORES REVISITED

YIELD: Varies

Tired of plain s'mores? Change up the chocolate type, use different types of cookies (Mint! Biscoff! Chocolate chip!), and slip in exciting add-ons (Strawberries! Banana slices! Citrus curd!). However, the jury is still very much out as to whether any changes can ultimately improve upon the original. But, if you just can't help but innovate, go ahead and try the parenthetical ideas or one of these two:

FOR THE S'MORES CONES

Sugar cones

Mini marshmallows

Chocolate chips

FOR THE S'MORES BUNS

Biscuit rolls

Marshmallows

Chocolate

Butter

Cinnamon sugar

Anything else you want to try in s'mores form!

S'MORES CONES

Stuff sugar cones (the kind you use for ice cream) with mini marshmallows and chocolate chips. Wrap each cone completely in aluminum foil. Place them on the grill over a medium campfire. Allow to heat, turning occasionally, for about 10 minutes or until the marshmallows and chocolate are melted and gooey. Unwrap and eat in all their sticky glory.

S'MORES BUNS

Here, a pack of premade biscuits works just as well as, or better than, homemade biscuit dough, but you could work with either. Take 8 biscuit rounds and flatten them until they are about ¼ inch (6 mm) thick. Wrap each around a full-size marshmallow and piece of chocolate, pinching the edges tightly together so nothing falls out. Heat a large cast-iron pan over the fire and melt in about 2 tablespoons (28 g) of butter. Add the stuffed biscuits and cook them in plenty of butter, turning the stuffed biscuits over and onto their sides every couple of minutes until they are cooked through and the centers are melted. If you want to get completely ridiculous, you can roll the finished buns in cinnamon sugar before eating, thereby creating something akin to a cinnamon sugar doughnut hole filled with chocolate and marshmallow.

Bananas still in their skins

Assorted fillings (see below)

Aluminum foil

BANANA BOATS

YIELD: Varies

You could camp without making banana boats, but are you really camping then? Banana boats are a camping dessert that is *alllllmost* as classic as s'mores. And they are equally fun and sticky.

1. Cut a slit down the middle of each banana, making sure you don't pierce through the skin on the bottom. Stuff the slit full of the filling combination of your choice (see below), then wrap your banana in 2 layers of aluminum foil.

2. Place the foil-wrapped bananas on a grate over the fire or settle them directly on dying embers. Cook until the bananas are soft and the fillings are melted, about 15 to 20 minutes.

3. Use long tongs to take the bananas off the fire, allow the aluminum to cool for just a minute, then unwrap the bananas and enjoy them while they are still a hot, sticky mess.

FILLING COMBINATIONS

The Classic: chocolate chips and mini marshmallows (or regular marshmallows torn to bits)

The Bananas Foster (for Adults Only!): brown sugar, a pat of butter, and a small spoonful of rum or bourbon

The Banana Split: chocolate chips, sliced strawberries, and canned pineapple bits

The Tropical: marshmallow bits, canned pineapple bits, and toasted shredded coconut

The Sticky Bun: caramel sauce, toasted pecans, and a sprinkle of sea salt

The PB: peanut butter, honey, and graham cracker bits

CAMPFIRE BANANAS FOSTER

YIELD: 4 servings

In reality this is far more dessert than fruit. And that's what makes it wonderful. You can serve these on their own, or if you have ice cream, yogurt, or heavy cream on hand, they are great with something creamy.

4 tablespoons (55 g) butter

4 tablespoons (60 g) brown sugar

4 bananas, sliced into ½-inch (1 cm) rounds

Wedge of lemon (optional)

1. Place a large skillet over a medium-low fire. Add the butter and allow to melt. Then stir in the sugar until it is mostly dissolved.

2. Add the banana slices and cook for a couple of minutes on the first side, gently shaking the pan to prevent them from sticking. Then flip and cook for a couple more minutes on the second side until the sugar and butter have formed a caramel sauce that coats the bananas. If desired, squeeze a little lemon over them to make all the flavors pop.

TIP

For another serving suggestion aside from ice cream, yogurt, or heavy cream: Thinly slice some plain angel food cake or pound cake and spoon some of the bananas Foster over each slice.

LODGE

4 medium-sized ripe but firm pears

Juice of 1 lemon

4 tablespoons (55 g) butter, softened

¼ cup (50 g) sugar

1 teaspoon vanilla extract

Aluminum foil

FOIL-PACK PEARS

YIELD: 4 to 8 servings

Pears are a subtle fruit. An understated fruit. A sometimes overlooked fruit. In the dessert realm, apples and berries get most of the attention, with an occasional nod to peaches in season. But pears deserve their moments to shine as well. When baked or roasted, their flavors concentrate and become almost candylike. Bathed with a bit of butter and sugar, they are remarkable. Tender and just sweet enough, they are satisfying as a dessert when you've maybe already had plenty to eat. You can also use them as an accompaniment for crepes or ice cream.

1. Cut each of the pears in half lengthwise and carefully cut or scoop out the cores, keeping each half intact. Then sprinkle the halves with lemon juice.

2. In a small bowl, combine the butter, sugar, and vanilla extract into something of a creamy paste. Smear this paste as best as you can on 4 pear halves. Then, place the other half of each pear on top, sandwiching the sugar mixture in between.

3. Wrap each pear tightly in a double layer of aluminum foil. Cook nestled directly in low coals, or on a grill over medium coals. Cook, turning occasionally, until the pears feel soft and squishy, about 30 to 40 minutes depending on the size of your pears. When soft, remove from the fire, carefully unwrap, and serve warm.

DUTCH OVEN APPLE CAKE

YIELD: 6 to 8 servings

Simple, rustic, redolent with cinnamon and apples, and perfect for eating in handheld wedges, this general recipe is adaptable to other chopped fruits as well. Think peaches, pears, or berries.

1. In a medium bowl, mix together the flour, baking soda, cinnamon, and salt.

2. In another bowl, whisk together the oil and sugar; then add the egg and whisk until smooth. Stir in the flour mixture until just incorporated (the batter will be thick). Then, fold in the apples. The apples will add some moisture and make the batter easier to stir.

3. Line a 10-inch (25 cm) Dutch oven with parchment paper, cutting down the paper to make sure it doesn't hang over the edges. Grease the parchment paper with butter or cooking spray, then spread the cake batter into the Dutch oven.

4. Cover the Dutch oven with its lid and place it on a grate over medium-high coals, or on top of a ring of coals on a heat-resistant surface. Shovel more coals on top of the Dutch oven. Allow the cake to bake until cooked through (you can carefully remove the lid using long tongs or a lid remover and use a knife or long skewer to test the cake for doneness), around 20 minutes. You will want to add fresh hot coals to the bottom and top of the Dutch oven at least once halfway through this process.

5. When the cake is done, use long tongs to remove the coals from the lid and remove the Dutch oven from the heat. Take off the lid and allow the cake to cool enough to touch it. Then serve.

1 cup (128 g) flour

½ teaspoon baking soda

1 teaspoon ground cinnamon

¼ teaspoon salt

¼ cup (59 ml) vegetable oil or olive oil

1 cup (200 g) granulated sugar

1 egg

2 cups (250 g) chopped tart apple (peel before chopping if you want)

Parchment paper

Butter or cooking spray for greasing the pan

1 cup (125 g) flour

1½ teaspoons (7 g) baking powder

½ teaspoon salt

1 cup (200 g) sugar

8 tablespoons (112 g) butter

1 cup (237 ml) whole milk

1 teaspoon vanilla

2 cups (290 g) fresh blueberries

CAMPFIRE COBBLER

YIELD: 6 to 8 servings

This recipe creates a cakelike dessert without needing a Dutch oven. The butter melted into the pan before adding the batter will seep over the sides of the pan, creating an amazing caramelized crispy chewiness while the berries cook into intense pops of flavor—yet the center stays soft and barely set.

1. Whisk together the flour, baking powder, salt, and sugar. This step can also be done at home and the premixed dry ingredients can be packed in a sealed container for transport to camp.

2. Place a 9-inch (23 cm) heavy-bottomed heat-resistant skillet (such as cast iron) on a grate over a campfire that has burned down to hot embers (or place the grate off to the side of an active fire). Add the stick of butter to the skillet and allow it to melt completely.

3. Add the milk and vanilla to the dry ingredients and stir together until smooth. With big oven mitts or heat-resistant leather gloves, grab the pan handle and swirl the hot pan with the butter to make sure it is fully coating the pan in a thick layer. Pour in the batter you made. As the batter sloshes into the pan, the butter will creep up all around the edges and over the top of the batter in some places.

4. Scatter the blueberries over the top of the batter, cover, and cook until the batter has just barely set in the middle, around 35 minutes. The bottom will most likely get burned (I don't think I've ever not burned it), but we all really like the burned bottom because it is deliciously caramelized from the butter.

5. Remove the cobbler from the fire and serve warm.

CAMPFIRE MONKEY BREAD

YIELD: 8 servings

Monkey bread is so sweet, gooey, and altogether irresistible. This foil-grilled version is great for outdoor cooking. It's surprisingly easy to whip up, and it's incredibly crowd-pleasing.

1 can of 8 biscuits

¼ cup (50 g) granulated sugar

1 teaspoon ground cardamom

½ teaspoon ground cinnamon

¼ cup (55 g) butter, cut into small pats

½ cup (115 g) light brown sugar

Aluminum foil

1. Combine the granulated sugar, cardamom, and cinnamon in a small bowl. Divide the biscuit dough into 32 pieces and roll each in the spiced sugar to coat it.

2. Make 2 aluminum foil rectangles, sprinkle any remaining sugar-spice mixture onto them, and divide the dough pieces between the foil pieces. Scatter the butter over the dough pieces and evenly sprinkle over the brown sugar. Then fold the foil tightly shut into packets. Feel free to wrap each in a second piece of foil if they don't seem tightly sealed enough to keep in melting sugar and butter.

3. Grill the packets over medium coals, flipping occasionally, until the biscuit pieces are cooked through and coated with a buttery sugar-caramel sauce, about 20 to 30 minutes. Remove the packets from the grill and allow the monkey breads to cool enough so that no one will scald their mouth on hot sugar (hot sugar is *very* hot). Then dig in.

SOFT CHOCOLATE COOKIES

YIELD: 1 dozen cookies

Try using these cookies with toasted marshmallows between to make a sort of devil's food/whoopee pie s'more situation. They are also amazing for snacking, or for making decadent ice cream sandwiches when you are at home. The combination of salt and chocolate is irresistible.

6 tablespoons (85 g) butter, softened

¾ cup (170 g) light brown sugar

1 egg

1 teaspoon vanilla extract

1 cup (125 g) flour

⅓ cup (29 g) cocoa powder

½ teaspoon baking soda

¼ teaspoon salt

1 tablespoon (15 ml) whole milk

Flaky salt for sprinkling

1. Preheat the oven to 350°F (180°C, or gas mark 4). In the bowl of a stand mixer fitted with a paddle attachment (or using a hand mixer), cream the butter and brown sugar together until lightened in color, about 3 minutes. Add the egg and beat in until fully incorporated. Mix in the vanilla extract.

2. In a small bowl, sift together the flour, cocoa powder, baking soda, and salt. Add the dry ingredients to the butter-sugar mixture and mix on low speed until almost fully combined. Add the milk and continue to mix just until everything is a uniform color and texture.

3. Scoop the dough into rounded tablespoon-sized balls and place onto a baking sheet. Sprinkle each with a small pinch of flaky salt. Bake for 9 to 10 minutes until they look puffed and dry on top but are still very pillowy and soft to the touch. Remove from the oven, transfer to a cooling rack, and allow to cool completely. (Okay, yes, you probably want to snack on one while it's still warm.) Transfer the cookies into an airtight container to pack for camping.

FLASK OLD-FASHIONED

YIELD: Varies

The appeal of this cocktail is clearly undeniable. The old-fashioned really epitomizes what good cocktails are all about: good ingredients adding up to more than the sum of their parts. In this case, the simple combination of whiskey, sugar, and bitters is balanced, satisfying, and enduring.

FOR 1 COCKTAIL

2 ounces (60 ml) whiskey

1 teaspoon simple syrup

3 to 4 dashes Angostura bitters

FOR AN 8-OUNCE (240 ML) FLASK

6 ounces (180 ml) whiskey

3 teaspoons simple syrup

12 dashes Angostura bitters

1¾ ounces (53 ml) water

FOR A 32-OUNCE (960 ML) WATER BOTTLE

3 cups (710 ml) whiskey

2 ounces (60 ml) simple syrup

About 5 teaspoons Angostura bitters

7 ounces (210 ml) water

FOR 1 COCKTAIL

Combine all the ingredients in a stirring glass and add ice. Stir to chill, then strain into a lowball glass over an ice cube.

FOR AN 8-OUNCE (240 ML) FLASK

Stir all the ingredients together in a small pitcher or measuring cup. Funnel all that fits into a flask. You should have just a wee bit left over to sip as a treat for doing such a good job making a flask cocktail.

FOR A 32-OUNCE (960 ML) WATER BOTTLE

Stir all the ingredients together in a pitcher. Pour all, or all that fits, into the water bottle.

APPLE NEGRONI

YIELD: Varies

The combination of gin, Campari, and sweet vermouth is undeniably a classic. It's also undeniably not very good at room temperature. The interplay of gin and Campari is too harsh when it isn't perfectly chilled. So what's a Negroni-loving person to do for their camping trips? The solution is simple: Make one of the many Negroni variations that use an aged base spirit. This particular variation uses apple brandy as the base spirit, which makes for a lusciously soft cocktail without being overtly fruity.

FOR 1 COCKTAIL

2 ounces (60 ml) Calvados or apple brandy

1 ounce (30 ml) Campari

1 ounce (30 ml) sweet vermouth

1 ounce (30 ml) water

FOR AN 8-OUNCE (240 ML) FLASK

3½ ounces (105 ml) Calvados or apple brandy

1¾ ounces (53 ml) Campari

1¾ ounces (53 ml) sweet vermouth

1¾ ounces (53 ml) water

FOR A 32-OUNCE (960 ML) WATER BOTTLE

12½ ounces (375 ml) Calvados or apple brandy

6¼ ounces (188 ml) Campari

6¼ ounces (188 ml) sweet vermouth

6¼ ounces (188 ml) water

FOR 1 COCKTAIL

Combine all the ingredients in a stirring glass and add ice. Stir to chill, then strain into a lowball glass over an ice cube.

FOR AN 8-OUNCE (240 ML) FLASK

Stir all the ingredients together in a small pitcher or measuring cup. Funnel all that fits into a flask. You should have just a wee bit left over to sip as a treat for doing such a good job making a flask cocktail.

FOR A 32-OUNCE (960 ML) WATER BOTTLE

Stir all the ingredients together in a pitcher. Pour all, or all that fits, into the water bottle.

SHETLAND SWEATER

YIELD: Varies

Scotland is renowned for its whiskey. It's a drink that's both comforting and complex, perfect for chilly nights or whenever you need a little extra warmth in your glass.

FOR 1 COCKTAIL

Combine all the ingredients in a stirring glass and add ice. Stir to chill, then strain into a lowball glass over an ice cube.

FOR AN 8-OUNCE (240 ML) FLASK

Stir all the ingredients together in a small pitcher or measuring cup. Funnel all that fits into a flask. You should have just a wee bit left over to sip as a treat for doing such a good job making a flask cocktail.

FOR A 32-OUNCE (960 ML) WATER BOTTLE

Stir all the ingredients together in a pitcher. Pour all, or all that fits, into the water bottle.

FOR 1 COCKTAIL

1 ounce (30 ml) blended Scotch

½ ounce (15 ml) apple brandy

½ ounce (15 ml) Amaro Averna

½ ounce (15 ml) Amaro Nonino

½ teaspoon maple syrup

1 dash orange bitters

A generous ½ ounce (15 ml) water

FOR AN 8-OUNCE (240 ML) FLASK

3 ounces (90 ml) blended Scotch

1½ ounces (45 ml) apple brandy

1½ ounces (45 ml) Amaro Averna

1½ ounces (45 ml) Amaro Nonino

1½ teaspoons (8 ml) maple syrup

2 dashes orange bitters

1½ ounces (45 ml) water

FOR A 32-OUNCE (960 ML) WATER BOTTLE

10½ ounces (315 ml) blended Scotch

5¼ ounces (158 ml) apple brandy

5¼ ounces (158 ml) Amaro Averna

5¼ ounces (158 ml) Amaro Nonino

¾ ounce (23 ml) maple syrup

6 dashes orange bitter

5¼ ounces (158 ml) water

FLASK RED RUM

YIELD: Varies

This is a spin-off of a cocktail called the Preakness, which is itself a spin-off of a Manhattan. Don't let the spinning make you dizzy; it's really a lovely balance of sweet and stiff between the spirits, vermouth, and liqueur. What makes it special is the rum and Tiki bitters, which give it a hint of the tropics. Just the smallest whiff of beachy escapism while you are on trail, you might say.

FOR 1 COCKTAIL

1 ounce (30 ml) rye whiskey

1 ounce (30 ml) aged rum

¾ ounce (23 ml) sweet vermouth

¼ ounce (8 ml) Bénédictine

4 dashes Tiki bitters

FOR AN 8-OUNCE (240 ML) FLASK

2 ounces (60 ml) rye whiskey

2 ounces (60 ml) aged rum

1½ ounces (45 ml) sweet vermouth

½ ounce (15 ml) Bénédictine

8 dashes Tiki bitters

1 ounce (30 ml) water

FOR A 32-OUNCE (960 ML) WATER BOTTLE

8 ounces (240 ml) rye whiskey

8 ounces (240 ml) aged rum

6 ounces (180 ml) sweet vermouth

2 ounces (60 ml) Bénédictine

5 teaspoons Tiki bitters

4 ounces (120 ml) water

FOR 1 COCKTAIL

Stir all the ingredients in a mixing glass with ice until chilled. Strain into a cocktail coupe. If desired, garnish with a lemon twist.

FOR AN 8-OUNCE (240 ML) FLASK

Stir all the ingredients together in a measuring cup or small pitcher and funnel into a flask.

FOR A 32-OUNCE (960 ML) WATER BOTTLE

Stir all the ingredients together in a large measuring cup or pitcher and pour into a water bottle.

INDEX

A

almond butter: Almond Butter Wrap with Dried Fruit and Cinnamon, 45
almonds: Trail Mix #1: Twist on Traditional, 57
Amaro Averna: Shetland Sweater, 120–121
Amaro Nonino: Shetland Sweater, 120–121
Angostura bitters: Flask Old-Fashioned, 116
apples
- Almond Butter Wrap with Dried Fruit and Cinnamon, 45
- Dutch Oven Apple Cake, 108
- Farmer's Lunch Sandwich, 38
- Trail Mix #3: Chunky Monkey, 61

apricots
- Almond Butter Wrap with Dried Fruit and Cinnamon, 45
- Grilled Bread with Toppings, 64

arugula: Turkey and Guacamole Wrap, 42
avocados
- Chilaquiles, 27
- Easy Breakfast Quesadillas, 20
- Grilled Bread with Toppings, 64
- Grilled Chicken Fajita Kebabs, 87

B

bacon: Cod Wrapped in Bacon, 95
bagels: Smoked Salmon and Bagel Sandwich, 41
bananas
- Campfire Bananas Foster, 104
- Trail Mix #3: Chunky Monkey, 61

barbecue sauce: Perfect T-Bone Steak, 80
beans. *See specific types*
beef
- Campfire Irish Stew, 71
- Perfect T-Bone Steak, 78–79
- Pie Iron Chimichangas, 75

beer
- Campfire Irish Stew, 71
- Chicken from Hell, 91

bell peppers
- Cod Wrapped in Bacon, 95
- Cream Cheese and Bell Pepper Frittata, 24
- Fish Curry, 92–93
- Forest Leczó (Hungarian Stew), 72
- Grilled Chicken Fajita Kebabs, 87
- Paella with Chorizo, 68
- Perfect T-Bone Steak, 80

Bénédictine: Flask Red Rum, 123
biscuits
- Campfire Monkey Bread, 112
- S'mores Revisited, 100

black beans: Campfire Nachos, 76
black olives: Campfire Nachos, 76
blueberries
- Campfire Cobbler, 111
- Just-Add-Water Pancakes, 28
- Maple-Blueberry Fruit Leather, 54

bourbon: Banana Boats, 103
brandy
- Apple Negroni, 119
- Shetland Sweater, 120–121

bread
- Chickpea Salad with Pita, 46
- Eggs in Purgatory, 23
- Farmer's Lunch Sandwich, 38
- Grilled Bread with Toppings, 64
- Herb-Crusted Cod, 96–97
- Pie Iron Chicken Potpies, 88
- Summer Sausage Sandwich, 37

C

Campari: Apple Negroni, 119
capicola: Summer Sausage Sandwich, 37
caramel sauce: Banana Boats, 103
carrots
- Campfire Irish Stew, 71
- Herb-Crusted Cod, 96–97
- Pie Iron Chicken Potpies, 88

celery
- Campfire Irish Stew, 71
- Pie Iron Chicken Potpies, 88

chai: French Press Dirty Chai, 31
cheddar cheese
- Campfire Nachos, 76
- Easy Breakfast Quesadillas, 20
- Farmer's Lunch Sandwich, 38
- Pie Iron Chimichangas, 75
- Summer Sausage Sandwich, 37

cheese. *See specific types*
cherries: Cherry-Pecan Granola, 16
chicken
- Campfire Nachos, 76
- Chicken from Hell, 91
- Grilled Chicken Fajita Kebabs, 87
- Paella with Chorizo, 68
- Pie Iron Chicken Potpies, 88

chickpeas: Chickpea Salad with Pita, 46
chiles
Chicken from Hell, 91
Fish Curry, 92–93
Perfect T-Bone Steak, 80
Sticky Pork Belly, 83
chocolate
Banana Boats, 103
Camper's Cookies, 53
S'mores Revisited, 100
Soft Chocolate Cookies, 115
Trail Mix #1: Twist on Traditional, 57
Trail Mix #3: Chunky Monkey, 61
chorizo: Paella with Chorizo, 68
ciabatta rolls
Curried Tuna Salad, 34
Grilled Bread with Toppings, 64
Summer Sausage Sandwich, 37
cinnamon
Almond Butter Wrap with Dried Fruit and Cinnamon, 45
Camper's Cookies, 53
Campfire Monkey Bread, 112
Cherry-Pecan Granola, 16
Dutch Oven Apple Cake, 108
Granola Bars, 50
S'mores Revisited, 100
coconut
Banana Boats, 103
Camper's Cookies, 53
Coconut Oatmeal Bowl, 19
Fish Curry, 92–93
cod
Cod Wrapped in Bacon, 95
Fish Curry, 92–93
Herb-Crusted Cod, 96–97
coffee: French Press Dirty Chai, 31
coppa
Grilled Bread with Toppings, 64
Summer Sausage Sandwich, 37
corn chips: Campfire Nachos, 76
crackers: Trail Mix #2: Kinda Fancy, 58
craisins: Trail Mix #3: Chunky Monkey, 61
cranberries: Trail Mix #1: Twist on Traditional, 57
cream cheese
Cream Cheese and Bell Pepper Frittata, 24
Smoked Salmon and Bagel Sandwich, 41
cucumbers
Chickpea Salad with Pita, 46
Cod Wrapped in Bacon, 95
currants: Just-Add-Water Pancakes, 28
curry powder
Curried Tuna Salad, 34
Fish Curry, 92–93

D

dates
Almond Butter Wrap with Dried Fruit and Cinnamon, 45
Granola Bars, 50

E

eggs
Camper's Cookies, 53
Chilaquiles, 27
Cream Cheese and Bell Pepper Frittata, 24
Dutch Oven Apple Cake, 108
Easy Breakfast Quesadillas, 20
Eggs in Purgatory, 23
Forest Leczó (Hungarian Stew), 72
Herb-Crusted Cod, 96–97
Soft Chocolate Cookies, 115

F

figs: Almond Butter Wrap with Dried Fruit and Cinnamon, 45

G

garlic
Campfire Irish Stew, 71
Chicken from Hell, 91
Chickpea Salad with Pita, 46
Fish Curry, 92–93
Forest Leczó (Hungarian Stew), 72
Grilled Chicken Fajita Kebabs, 87
Herb-Crusted Cod, 96–97
Paella with Chorizo, 68
Perfect T-Bone Steak, 78–79
Pie Iron Chicken Potpies, 88
Sticky Pork Belly, 83
ginger
Fish Curry, 92–93
Sticky Pork Belly, 83
Goldfish crackers: Trail Mix #2: Kinda Fancy, 58
graham crackers: Banana Boats, 103
guacamole
Easy Breakfast Quesadillas, 20
Turkey and Guacamole Wrap, 42
guava: Coconut Oatmeal Bowl, 19
Guinness: Campfire Irish Stew, 71

H

honey
Banana Boats, 103
Chicken from Hell, 91
Granola Bars, 50
Grilled Bread with Toppings, 64
Perfect T-Bone Steak, 80
Sticky Pork Belly, 83

J

Jack cheese
Campfire Nachos, 76
Easy Breakfast Quesadillas, 20
jalapeño peppers
Campfire Nachos, 76
Chicken from Hell, 91

K

kielbasa: Forest Leczó (Hungarian Stew), 72
kiwi: Coconut Oatmeal Bowl, 19

L

lamb
Campfire Irish Stew, 71
Lamb Chops with Pomegranate Sauce, 84

lemons
Campfire Bananas Foster, 104
Chicken from Hell, 91
Chickpea Salad with Pita, 46
Cod Wrapped in Bacon, 95
Curried Tuna Salad, 34
Foil-Pack Pears, 107
Granola Bars, 50
Herb-Crusted Cod, 96–97
Maple-Blueberry Fruit Leather, 54
Paella with Chorizo, 68
Pita or Naan Pizzas, 67
lettuce
Farmer's Lunch Sandwich, 38
Smoked Salmon and Bagel Sandwich, 41
Turkey and Guacamole Wrap, 42
limes
Fish Curry, 92–93
Grilled Chicken Fajita Kebabs, 87
Herb-Crusted Cod, 96–97

M

mango: Coconut Oatmeal Bowl, 19
maple syrup
Cherry-Pecan Granola, 16
French Press Dirty Chai, 31
Just-Add-Water Pancakes, 28
Maple-Blueberry Fruit Leather, 54
Shetland Sweater, 120–121
marinara sauce: Eggs in Purgatory, 23
marshmallows
Banana Boats, 103
S'mores Revisited, 100
mayonnaise
Curried Tuna Salad, 34
Farmer's Lunch Sandwich, 38
Turkey and Guacamole Wrap, 42
M&Ms: Camper's Cookies, 53
Monterey Jack cheese: Easy Breakfast Quesadillas, 20
mozzarella cheese
Chicken from Hell, 91
Pita or Naan Pizzas, 67
mustard
Farmer's Lunch Sandwich, 38
Herb-Crusted Cod, 96–97

N

naan bread: Pita or Naan Pizzas, 67
nori: Trail Mix #2: Kinda Fancy, 58

O

oats
Camper's Cookies, 53
Cherry-Pecan Granola, 16
Coconut Oatmeal Bowl, 19
Granola Bars, 50
olive oil
Cherry-Pecan Granola, 16
Chickpea Salad with Pita, 46
Cod Wrapped in Bacon, 95
Cream Cheese and Bell Pepper Frittata, 24
Dutch Oven Apple Cake, 108
Granola Bars, 50
Grilled Bread with Toppings, 64
Grilled Chicken Fajita Kebabs, 87
Lamb Chops with Pomegranate Sauce, 84
Paella with Chorizo, 68
Perfect T-Bone Steak, 78–79
Pita or Naan Pizzas, 67
Sticky Pork Belly, 83
Trail Mix #1: Twist on Traditional, 57
Trail Mix #3: Chunky Monkey, 61
olives
Campfire Nachos, 76
Pita or Naan Pizzas, 67
onions
Campfire Irish Stew, 71
Campfire Nachos, 76
Chicken from Hell, 91
Chickpea Salad with Pita, 46
Cod Wrapped in Bacon, 95
Cream Cheese and Bell Pepper Frittata, 24
Fish Curry, 92–93
Forest Leczó (Hungarian Stew), 72
Grilled Chicken Fajita Kebabs, 87
Herb-Crusted Cod, 96–97
Paella with Chorizo, 68
Perfect T-Bone Steak, 80
Pie Iron Chicken Potpies, 88
orange bitters: Shetland Sweater, 120–121

P

paella rice: Paella with Chorizo, 68
Parmesan cheese: Herb-Crusted Cod, 96–97
parsnips: Herb-Crusted Cod, 96–97
peaches: Almond Butter Wrap with Dried Fruit and Cinnamon, 45
peanut butter
Banana Boats, 103
Granola Bars, 50
Trail Mix #3: Chunky Monkey, 61
pears: Foil-Pack Pears, 107
peas
Paella with Chorizo, 68
Pie Iron Chicken Potpies, 88
pecans
Banana Boats, 103
Camper's Cookies, 53
Cherry-Pecan Granola, 16
Trail Mix #1: Twist on Traditional, 57
pepperoni: Pita or Naan Pizzas, 67
pickles: Farmer's Lunch Sandwich, 38
pineapple
Banana Boats, 103
Coconut Oatmeal Bowl, 19
Cod Wrapped in Bacon, 95
Perfect T-Bone Steak, 80
Pita or Naan Pizzas, 67
pitas
Chickpea Salad with Pita, 46
Pita or Naan Pizzas, 67
pizza sauce: Eggs in Purgatory, 23
Polish sausage: Forest Leczó (Hungarian Stew), 72
pomegranate: Lamb Chops with Pomegranate Sauce, 84
pork
Campfire Nachos, 76
Cod Wrapped in Bacon, 95
Forest Leczó (Hungarian Stew), 72

Grilled Bread with Toppings, 64
Perfect T-Bone Steak, 80
Pita or Naan Pizzas, 67
Sticky Pork Belly, 83
Summer Sausage Sandwich, 37
potatoes
Campfire Irish Stew, 71
Lamb Chops with Pomegranate Sauce, 84
Perfect T-Bone Steak, 78–79
pretzels: Trail Mix #3: Chunky Monkey, 61
prosciutto
Grilled Bread with Toppings, 64
Pita or Naan Pizzas, 67
Summer Sausage Sandwich, 37
prunes: Almond Butter Wrap with Dried Fruit and Cinnamon, 45

Q

queso fresco: Chilaquiles, 27

R

raisins
Camper's Cookies, 53
Curried Tuna Salad, 34
Trail Mix #1: Twist on Traditional, 57
Trail Mix #3: Chunky Monkey, 61
refried beans: Pie Iron Chimichangas, 75
rice
Fish Curry, 92–93
Paella with Chorizo, 68
ricotta cheese: Grilled Bread with Toppings, 64
rum
Banana Boats, 103
Flask Red Rum, 123

S

saffron: Paella with Chorizo, 68
salmon
Grilled Bread with Toppings, 64
Smoked Salmon and Bagel Sandwich, 41
sausage
Forest Leczó (Hungarian Stew), 72
Summer Sausage Sandwich, 37
scallions
Herb-Crusted Cod, 96–97
Perfect T-Bone Steak, 80
Smoked Salmon and Bagel Sandwich, 41
Scotch: Shetland Sweater, 120–121
seaweed: Trail Mix #2: Kinda Fancy, 58
sesame sticks: Trail Mix #2: Kinda Fancy, 58
shrimp: Paella with Chorizo, 68
sourdough bread: Grilled Bread with Toppings, 64
soy sauce: Sticky Pork Belly, 83
strawberries: Banana Boats, 103
summer sausage: Summer Sausage Sandwich, 37

T

tahini: Chickpea Salad with Pita, 46
Tiki bitters: Flask Red Rum, 123
tomatillos: Chilaquiles, 27
tomatoes
Campfire Nachos, 76
Chickpea Salad with Pita, 46
Chilaquiles, 27
Cod Wrapped in Bacon, 95
Easy Breakfast Quesadillas, 20
Farmer's Lunch Sandwich, 38
Fish Curry, 92–93
Forest Leczó (Hungarian Stew), 72
Grilled Bread with Toppings, 64
Paella with Chorizo, 68
Pie Iron Chimichangas, 75
Smoked Salmon and Bagel Sandwich, 41
Turkey and Guacamole Wrap, 42
tomato sauce
Forest Leczó (Hungarian Stew), 72
Pita or Naan Pizzas, 67
tortilla chips: Chilaquiles, 27
tortillas
Almond Butter Wrap with Dried Fruit and Cinnamon, 45
Easy Breakfast Quesadillas, 20
Grilled Chicken Fajita Kebabs, 87
Pie Iron Chimichangas, 75
Turkey and Guacamole Wrap, 42
trout: Grilled Bread with Toppings, 64
tuna: Curried Tuna Salad, 34
turkey: Turkey and Guacamole Wrap, 42

V

vegetable stock: Fish Curry, 92–93
vermouth
Apple Negroni, 119
Flask Red Rum, 123

W

walnuts: Trail Mix #3: Chunky Monkey, 61
wasabi peas: Trail Mix #2: Kinda Fancy, 58
whiskey
Flask Old-Fashioned, 116
Flask Red Rum, 123
Perfect T-Bone Steak, 78–79
Sticky Pork Belly, 83
wine
Campfire Irish Stew, 71
Cod Wrapped in Bacon, 95
Lamb Chops with Pomegranate Sauce, 84
Pie Iron Chicken Potpies, 88

Y

yams: Chickpea Salad with Pita, 46

Z

zucchini
Forest Leczó (Hungarian Stew), 72
Herb-Crusted Cod, 96–97

ALSO AVAILABLE

Smoking
978-0-7603-9745-9

Grilling
978-0-7603-9747-3

Griddling
978-1-57715-654-3

Rice Cooker
978-0-7603-9741-1

Slow Cooker
978-1-57715-658-1

Bread Machine
978-1-57715-660-4

Air Fryer
978-0-7603-9743-5